WEEKENDS FOR TWO IN NEW ENGLAND

Weekends for Two in
NEW ENGLAND

50 Romantic Getaways

BY BILL GLEESON

PHOTOGRAPHS BY CARY HAZLEGROVE

CHRONICLE BOOKS

SAN FRANCISCO

CONTENTS

ACKNOWLEDGMENTS

The author and photographer wish to thank the following individuals for their contributions, inspiration, and support:

Yvonne Gleeson, research assistance
Andy Bullington, Lucy Hazlegrove, Julie Hunsaker, Ann Schmidt, Robert and Ferne Gleeson, Richard and Isabel Gomes

Cover Photo: The Boulders, New Preston, CT

Text copyright © 1996 by Bill Gleeson.
Photographs copyright © 1996 by Cary Hazlegrove.

Printed in Hong Kong.

Book design by Robin Weiss.

Library of Congress Cataloging-in-Publication Data:

Gleeson, Bill.
    Weekends for two in New England: 50 romantic getaways / Bill Gleeson; photographs by Cary Hazlegrove.
        p. cm.
    Includes index.
    ISBN 0-8118-0857-2 (pbk.)
    1. Hotels—New England—Guidebooks. 2. Bed and breakfast accommodations—New England—Guidebooks. 3. New England—Guidebooks. I. Title.
TX907.3.N35G58 1995
647.947401—dc20   95-12146
                                        CIP

Distributed in Canada by
Raincoast Books,
8680 Cambie Street, Vancouver, B.C.
V6P 6M9

10 9 8 7 6 5 4 3 2 1

Chronicle Books
275 Fifth Street
San Francisco, CA 94103

INTRODUCTION

*W*hoever coined the adage "Home is where the heart is" neglected to mention that home is also where the chores, children, telephones, and pots and pans are. Let's face it: there are times when the heart, at least the romantic part, needs a change of scene.

And because romantic respites from parenting, dual careers, cooking, and cleaning come all too infrequently, choosing a suitably romantic destination is probably the most important decision you'll make when planning a cherished weekend away.

Unfortunately, our choices are often a blind leap of faith, based largely on recommendations from well-meaning friends, on self-serving brochures that stretch the definitions of "romantic" and "charming," or on guidebooks created by writers who never ventured beyond the lobby.

The concept for a discerning, dependable series of romantic travel guides was conceived after one too many unpleasant weekends in unappealing lodgings inaccurately portrayed by innkeepers and friends as "romantic." Armed with some specific criteria and a critical eye, we hit the road with the goal of separating romantic fact from fiction.

Selection

Our process of identifying New England's most romantic inns and small hotels wasn't completely scientific. For this volume, we considered recommendations from well-seasoned travel professionals whose opinions we respect, and then we conducted our own personal inn-to-inn searches along thousands of miles of highways and byways in six states: Maine, Vermont, New Hampshire, Massachusetts, Connecticut, and Rhode Island.

In narrowing our list to fifty, consideration was given to providing our readers with a range of accommodations in terms of rates, size, location, ambience, and setting. We visited each destination and toured or slept in literally hundreds of guest rooms.

Rooms for Romance

When evaluating the romantic appeal of a property, we consider the following criteria, honed through visits to destinations around the country. We look for:

- Private bathrooms (a must in our opinion; we tell you if any are shared)
- In-room fireplaces
- Tubs or showers designed for two
- Breakfast in bed
- Feather beds and cushy comforters
- Canopied, four-poster, king-sized beds
- Couches, love seats, or nooks for sitting together
- Private decks, patios, or balconies with inspirational views
- Romantic decor and special touches such as fresh flowers and music
- Properties in which smoking is not permitted

We also sought out small hotels and inns that exude that overall, sometimes difficult-to-describe intimate atmosphere that engenders romantic sparks. And while we've nothing against children (we have two of our own), we have come to appreciate policies that discourage younger visitors. Many couples are seeking a well-deserved break from the kids, and the (sometimes loud) evidence of little people in the room next door or in the hall doesn't exactly contribute to a passionate getaway.

Finally, we avoided destinations referred to in the lodging industry as homestays. These are houses in which a room or rooms are rented out to travelers, often by resident owners lacking skill in the art of innkeeping.

Within the inns and small hotels listed in this book, we discovered special rooms that are particularly conducive to a romantic experience. Instead of leaving the choice of rooms to the reservation clerk and describing in detail the public areas of each establishment, we've devoted a good part of this book to details of particularly romantic rooms and suites. When booking your getaway reservation, don't hesitate to ask about the availability of a specific room—especially if you already have a personal favorite.

Tables for Two

At the beginning of each regional listing, we've identified particularly noteworthy restaurants near our featured destinations. These were sampled by us and/or recommended by innkeepers whose opinions we respect. Keep in mind, however, that restaurants—and chefs—come and go. Accordingly, we suggest you balance these recommendations with updates and new choices offered by your innkeeper, who will be happy to offer suggestions.

Your Favorites

If we've overlooked one of your cherished romantic destinations, please write to us in care of Chronicle Books, 275 Fifth Street, San Francisco, CA 94103. We look forward to sharing new romantic weekends for two in future printings.

About Rates

Travelers scouting the East Coast highways for discount lodgings can still find a no-frills motel room for $50, but this guide isn't for bargain hunters. We view our romantic times together as the most special of occasions, and through years of travel we've confirmed that you really do get what you pay for. Consequently, you should understand that a special room usually commands a higher price. In fact, you'll find few rooms described in these pages for less than $100 per night.

Many of our featured destinations offer substantially reduced rates during mid-season and low-season, which vary widely by location. Also keep in mind that most of our recommended properties require two-night minimum stays during weekends and holidays.

To help you plan your getaway budget, approximate 1996 high-season weekend nightly rates for specific rooms are noted within each description. Rates (per night for two friendly people) are classified at the end of each listing in the following ranges, not including tax:

> Moderate: Under $150
> Expensive: $150-$200
> Deluxe: Over $200

Final Notes

No payment was sought or accepted from any establishment in exchange for a listing in this book.

Food, wine, and flowers were occasionally added to our photo scenes for styling purposes. Some inns provide these amenities; others do not. Please ask when making a reservation whether these items are complimentary or whether they're provided at an extra charge.

Also, please understand we cannot guarantee that these properties will maintain furnishings or standards as they existed on our visit, and we very much appreciate hearing from readers if their experience is at variance with our descriptions. Reader comments are carefully consulted in the creation and revision of each *Weekends for Two* volume. Your opinions are important.

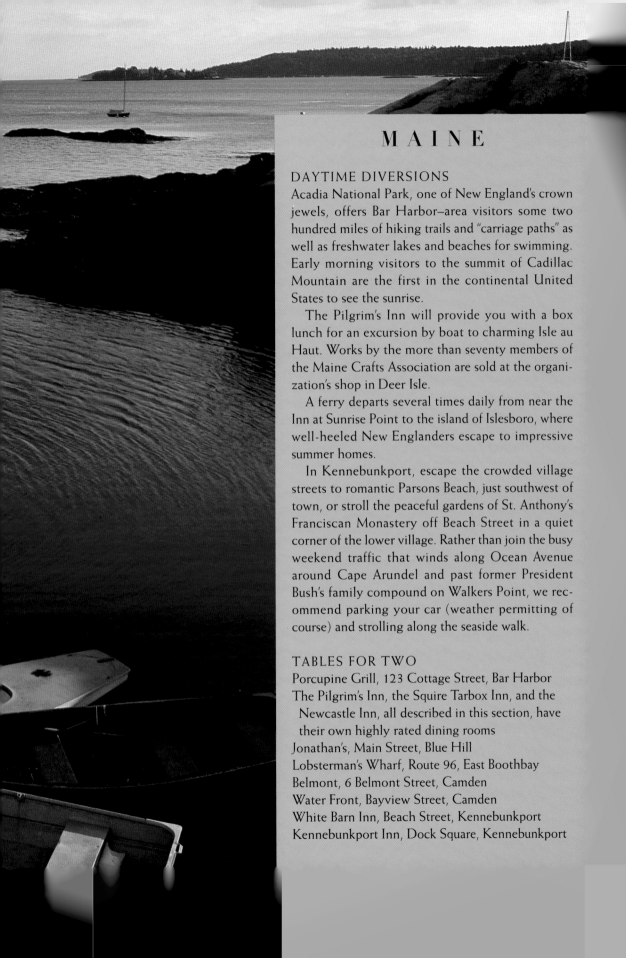

MAINE

DAYTIME DIVERSIONS

Acadia National Park, one of New England's crown jewels, offers Bar Harbor–area visitors some two hundred miles of hiking trails and "carriage paths" as well as freshwater lakes and beaches for swimming. Early morning visitors to the summit of Cadillac Mountain are the first in the continental United States to see the sunrise.

The Pilgrim's Inn will provide you with a box lunch for an excursion by boat to charming Isle au Haut. Works by the more than seventy members of the Maine Crafts Association are sold at the organization's shop in Deer Isle.

A ferry departs several times daily from near the Inn at Sunrise Point to the island of Islesboro, where well-heeled New Englanders escape to impressive summer homes.

In Kennebunkport, escape the crowded village streets to romantic Parsons Beach, just southwest of town, or stroll the peaceful gardens of St. Anthony's Franciscan Monastery off Beach Street in a quiet corner of the lower village. Rather than join the busy weekend traffic that winds along Ocean Avenue around Cape Arundel and past former President Bush's family compound on Walkers Point, we recommend parking your car (weather permitting of course) and strolling along the seaside walk.

TABLES FOR TWO

Porcupine Grill, 123 Cottage Street, Bar Harbor
The Pilgrim's Inn, the Squire Tarbox Inn, and the
  Newcastle Inn, all described in this section, have
  their own highly rated dining rooms
Jonathan's, Main Street, Blue Hill
Lobsterman's Wharf, Route 96, East Boothbay
Belmont, 6 Belmont Street, Camden
Water Front, Bayview Street, Camden
White Barn Inn, Beach Street, Kennebunkport
Kennebunkport Inn, Dock Square, Kennebunkport

BREAKWATER 1904

45 Hancock Street
Bar Harbor, ME 04609
Telephone: (207) 288-2313 or
 toll-free: (800) 238-6309

Six rooms, each with private bath and gas fireplace.
Complimentary full breakfast served in dining room
at huge communal table. No handicapped access.
Smoking is not permitted. Two-night minimum stay
required during high-season weekends and holiday
periods. Open Easter weekend through Veterans Day
weekend. Expensive to deluxe.

Getting There
From Interstate 95 at Bangor, take the Route 395
bypass to Route 1A and follow to Ellsworth (Route
1A becomes Route 3). Follow Route 3 into Bar Harbor
where it veers left onto Mount Desert Street. Turn
right on Main Street and drive three blocks to
Hancock Street. Turn left and follow to inn drive
on right.

BREAKWATER 1904
Bar Harbor

$\mathcal{G}$azing out over Frenchman Bay from an opulent bedroom high in this magnificent mansion from the gilded age, it occurred to us just how indebted we traveling romantics are to wealth and the comforts it can create. Were it not for the moneyed few who built indulgent residences that now function as cherished inns, our romantic getaway options would be sorely limited.

We're also thankful to folks like Breakwater's owners Tom and Bonnie Sawyer, who make such places accessible to couples who otherwise could only drive by and dream. Most of us will never live like this, but the Sawyers have made it possible to make believe for a night or two.

The stone-and-half-timbered "cottage," which stands at water's edge a couple of blocks from downtown Bar Harbor, was built just after the turn of the century as a summer retreat for the great-grandson of John Jacob Astor. When they restored the estate in the early 1990s, the Sawyers remained true to the structure's integrity. Instead of chopped up accommodations, guests luxuriate in grand original-sized bedrooms. Indeed, there are but six guest rooms in this regal mansion. All but one have great views of the bay and Bald Porcupine Island.

Rooms for Romance

In Mrs. Alsop's Chamber (upper $200 range), built-in cushioned deacon's benches face each other in front of the fireplace. The king-sized bed (the inn's only king bed) has oak head- and footboards. There's also a fluffy chaise in this second-floor corner, illuminated by six windows. The bathroom has a marble sink and a tiled shower stall.

Our room for a night was Ambassador Jay's Chamber (mid $200 range), a palatial room whose polished spruce floor was covered with Persian rugs. A couch and love seat were placed under three leaded, bay-view windows, and the gas fireplace was visible from the queen-sized four-poster bed. The vintage-style, honeycomb-tiled bathroom held an oak water closet and a small old-fashioned tub with a brass shower extension.

Offered in the upper $100 range, Abigail's Chamber, on the third floor, is the least expensive room in the house. Although lacking a water view, the room is a cheerful and generously sized hideaway, furnished with a queen-sized bed and two cushioned chairs. The pretty bathroom has a window seat and large tiled shower with a lovely stained-glass window.

A word of discretion: the home contains many interior doors that originally connected guest bedrooms, bathrooms, and common areas. Although these are now locked to ensure privacy, voices do carry.

Guests at Breakwater 1904 enjoy delightful walking access to downtown shops via a romantic walking path along the rocky shore past neighboring homes.

MANOR HOUSE INN

106 West Street
Bar Harbor, ME 04609
Telephone: (207) 288-3759

Fourteen rooms, each with private bath. Complimentary full breakfast served at tables for two in dining room. No handicapped access. Smoking is not permitted. Two-night minimum stay required during weekends and holiday periods. Closed from mid-November through mid-April. Moderate to expensive.

Getting There
From the Maine Turnpike at Bangor, take the Route 395 bypass to Route 1A and follow to Ellsworth (Route 1A becomes Route 3). Follow Route 3 into Bar Harbor. Turn left on West Street and follow to inn on right.

MANOR HOUSE INN

Bar Harbor

We felt so strongly about Bar Harbor's enchanting romantic appeal that we decided to include two blissful destinations here. Located just steps from the town's shopping area, Manor House Inn affords the two of you an opportunity to walk to the harbor, explore Bar Harbor without having to search for a parking place, and then curl up in a cozy, moderately priced guest room.

Situated in a neighborhood of historic homes, Manor House Inn is a three-story, gabled, shuttered, and bay-windowed mansion whose fine wraparound porch holds lots of comfy couches and chairs. Sharing the one-acre estate are the Chauffeur's Cottage (with three rooms) and two freestanding single cottages.

Rooms for Romance

Our favorite room is Suite A (mid $100 range) on the second floor of the refurbished, century-old Chauffeur's Cottage. The suite has a large carpeted sitting room with a Victorian couch and chair, a fireplace, and a wet bar. The big beautiful bedroom, set under skylit eaves, has a king-sized antique bed. The large bathroom has a tub-and-shower combination. A private deck faces the trees.

In the restored main house, which dates back to 1887, our first choice is Room 5 (low to mid $100 range), known as the Master Bedroom. This front-facing, second-floor corner holds a queen-sized bed, a chaise longue, and a fireplace. The large, bright bathroom has a shower and four windows.

Room 7 (low $100 range) is situated under the eaves on the third floor and has a small separate sitting room. There's a shower stall in the bathroom.

Travelers who value complete privacy should be advised that the assigned bathrooms of rooms 2, 4, and 8 in the main house are across the hall from their respective bed chambers. We don't recommend these rooms for romantic getaways. We did not have an opportunity to tour the two guest cottages, which carry tariffs of around $100.

JOHN PETERS INN

P.O. Box 916
Blue Hill, ME 04614
Telephone: (207) 374-2116

Fourteen rooms, each with private bath; nine with woodburning fireplaces. Canoe and rowboat are available to guests. Complimentary full breakfast served in bay-view breakfast room at tables for two or in your room. Swimming pool (not heated). Limited handicapped access. Smoking is not permitted. No minimum stay requirement. Closed November through April. Moderate to expensive.

Getting There
From Route 1, six miles east of the Bucksport bridge, drive south on Route 15 to Blue Hill. The inn is a half-mile north of the village just off Route 176 east.

JOHN PETERS INN
Blue Hill

When we recall our romantic New England travels, it's John Peters Inn, with its columned porch, its expanse of lawn that sweeps to Blue Hill Bay, and its cozy firelit rooms, that often springs first to mind. One of our favorite New England discoveries, this splendid Greek Revival mansion should rank as a must-stop on the itinerary of Maine-bound couples who savor comfort, quiet, and beauty.

But be forewarned. While many visiting romantics arrive with well-intentioned plans for excursions to nearby Penobscot Bay, Deer Isle, or Mount Desert Island, guests of John Peters Inn frequently lose motivation to move beyond their guest room or the inn's own twenty-five shorelined acres. Except for an evening trip into Blue Hill for dinner at Jonathan's or Firepond, there's little reason to leave.

Rooms for Romance

Our top pick is the Blue Hill Room (mid $100 range), a large second-floor room in the main house with a king-sized four-poster bed, a wet bar, a woodburning fireplace, and Oriental rug–covered wide pine floors. A romantic bonus is the glorious outdoor deck that overlooks Blue Hill Bay, the swimming pool, and the lawn. The bathroom has a large clawfoot tub and a separate shower stall.

Surry (mid $100 range) is another large, second-floor corner room with water views. This room boasts six windows on three sides, a king-sized bed, a couch, and a woodburning fireplace. There's a tub-and-shower combination in the bathroom.

For economy-minded travelers, there's Deer Isle (around $100), a second-floor room with a queen-sized bed, a love seat, and a view of the swimming pool. For just a few dollars more, you can reserve Penobscot, which offers a fireplace and a good view of the bay.

On the ground floor, Castine (mid $100 range) is a spacious room with windows on three sides. The bay is visible through branches of a tree. The nice bathroom holds an oversized tub with shower.

The remote Carriage House is a two-story shingled building housing six large rooms offered from the low to mid $100 range. Four of these are apartment-sized and are equipped with kitchens. All but two have country-view decks.

THE PILGRIM'S INN

Main Street
Deer Isle, ME 04627
Telephone: (207) 348-6615

Thirteen rooms, eight with private baths. Complimentary full breakfast served in dining room at communal table and tables for two. All rates include dinner for two. Handicapped access. Smoking is allowed. No minimum stay requirement. Moderate to deluxe.

Getting There
From the Maine Turnpike at Augusta, exit at Route 3 and drive northeast to Belfast, then follow Route 1 north to Route 15 south. Turn right on Route 15 south down the Blue Hill peninsula to Deer Isle, and turn right on Main Street (the Sunset Road). Drive one block to inn on left.

THE PILGRIM'S INN

Deer Isle

*E*ven though it doesn't require a ferry ride, Deer Isle offers visitors a taste of the same quiet, unspoiled atmosphere you'd expect at a more remote water-bound destination. Much of that atmosphere is provided by the venerable, two-century-old Pilgrim's Inn.

Just a short hop by bridge from the mainland, er, Maineland, the inn is a sturdy, gambrel-roofed structure with lots of cozy public rooms and the requisite old creaky floors, either polished or painted. The inn, which sports a rooster-red paint job, presides over Mill Pond and adjacent Northwest Harbor, and boasts a fine water-view lawn area with lots of places to enjoy quiet time together.

Highly rated dinners are included in the room rate and are served at tables for two in a rustic and handsome dining room paneled with ancient barn wood. Free rental bicycles are available to guests.

Rooms for Romance

Not every room fits our definition of romance since several otherwise enticing accommodations share bathrooms. Eight of the thirteen rooms have private baths. Rooms 9, 10, 11, 12, and 14 share.

Honeymooners and more seasoned romantic travelers request Room 5 (upper $100 range), a large rear corner that overlooks Mill Pond. A full-sized four-poster bed and two wing chairs sit on pumpkin-pine floors. The private bathroom has a tub that's equipped with a hand-held shower attachment.

Also popular is Room 8 (upper $100 range). This small, second-floor rear corner is furnished with painted-pine furniture and a full-sized bed. The bathroom has a tub-and-shower combination.

Room 15 (around $200) is a nearby village cottage operated by the inn that's also available for romantic getaways. On the first floor of the cottage is an open-beamed living room with a fireplace, a kitchen, a dining area, and a powder room. A bedroom and a bathroom are tucked away upstairs.

THE INN AT SUNRISE POINT

P.O. Box 1344
Camden, ME 04843
Telephone: (207) 236-7716 or
toll-free: (800) 237-8674

Seven rooms, each with private bath and woodburning fireplace. Complimentary full breakfast served at
tables of two or more or in your room. Handicapped
access. Smoking is not permitted. Two-night minimum
stay during holiday periods. Closed late October
through late May. Expensive to deluxe.

Getting There
From the Maine Turnpike, take exit 22 in Brunswick,
and follow Route 1 north through Camden. (Route 90
north of Waldoboro saves several miles and brings
you to Route 1 south of Camden.) Four miles north
of Camden Harbor, turn right off Route 1 onto Fire
Road 9 (FR-9) and follow to inn.

THE INN AT SUNRISE POINT

Camden

As the author of a series of popular bed-and-breakfast inn guides, Inn at Sunrise Point owner Jerry Levitin visited thousands of properties from coast to coast before building his own. He knows what works and what doesn't, and at Sunrise Point, everything works.

Jerry created his vision of the perfect luxury hideaway virtually from the ground up, starting with the perfect setting, a seaside clearing reached by a hidden fire road. He lavished appropriate attention on bathrooms, installing generous countertops of Corian tile, makeup mirrors, hair dryers, and tubs for two. In the bedrooms, there are comfy chairs, fireplaces, and comfortable beds positioned to take full advantage of unobstructed Penobscot Bay views. There's even soothing piped-in music with adjustable volume controls (except in the cottages) and televisions with videocassette players. Guests are also treated to plush robes and towels of Egyptian cotton.

The centerpiece of the downstairs public area is a spectacular glass conservatory, in which appetizers and full breakfasts are served before an ocean view.

Rooms for Romance

In the main house, there are three moderately sized upstairs rooms, each named after an author. These carry tariffs in the mid $100 range, and each has a woodburning fireplace, a queen-sized bed, and a bathroom with an extra-long tub big enough for two. The smallest is the middle room, called E. B. White. The May Sarton and Sarah Jewett rooms are nicely windowed corners.

The inn's ultimate accommodations are four luxurious cottages (around $300) set against the trees. These offer oval-shaped spa tubs for two, separate showers, wood-burning fireplaces, small refrigerators, coffeemakers, and private decks.

The Fitz Hugh Lane Cottage, situated only ten feet from the water's edge, boasts eye-popping bay views and is our personal favorite. It's furnished with two queen-sized beds. Winslow Homer, equipped with a king-sized bed, is considered the honeymoon cottage. The William Burpee Cottage is set back a bit farther on the property, but still has a nice bay view.

THE NEWCASTLE INN

River Road
Newcastle, ME 04553
Telephone: (207) 563-5685 or
toll-free: (800) 832-8669

Fifteen rooms, each with private bath. Complimentary full breakfast served in dining room at tables for four. Dinner included in rates. Restaurant. No handicapped access. Smoking is not permitted. No minimum stay requirement. Expensive.

Getting There
Take the Maine Turnpike (Interstate 95) to exit 22 (Bath/Brunswick/Coastal Route 1). Take Route 1 northeast; Newcastle is seven miles past Wiscasset. Turn right on River Road (watch for Newcastle Inn sign) and follow a half-mile to inn on right.

THE NEWCASTLE INN

Newcastle

*O*ur recommendation of The Newcastle Inn springs primarily from the reputation of its dining room as one of the finest—and of its hosts as among the most gracious—on the Maine coast. Despite the fact that certain rooms lack the sensual romantic appeal of others we've featured, this comfortable inn is certainly worthy of a stopover should your Maine travels bring you here.

Owned by Ted and Chris Sprague, the inn is a handsome Colonial-style clapboard home

painted white and bedecked with contrasting dark blue shutters. Looking resplendent after a complete renovation in the late 1980s, it stands on a gentle knoll overlooking the Damariscotta River.

Evenings at the inn begin with cocktail hour in a cozy red-walled pub, with complimentary hors d'oeuvres. A wonderful multicourse dinner follows, prepared by Chris and served at tables for two. Dinners and full breakfasts are included in the room rates. Dinners without a room are available at a fixed price of around $75 for two.

Rooms for Romance

At the time of our visit, rooms carried approximate high-season rates of $150, $170, and $190, depending primarily on size and location. Rates without dinner were around $60 less.

Room 8 (highest rate) is a rear third-floor corner with a queen-sized bed canopied in lace. Although the room has a cozy sitting area with a pair of chairs, there's no view from here. The large bathroom holds a tub-and-shower combination.

Room 9 (highest rate) occupies a small bright corner of the third floor where guests are treated to a river view. The queen-sized bed is made of brass and pewter, and the generously sized bathroom has a shower stall and a window. Room 7 (highest rate), another side-facing third-floor room, has a queen-sized sleigh bed.

In Room 6 (highest rate), the queen-sized canopied bed is placed diagonally to take advantage of a river view. A gas fireplace is situated between two windows. The small bathroom holds a tub-and-shower combination.

A private river-view deck is part of Room 11's charm. The queen-sized bed is partially canopied, and the small bathroom has a shower. This is also one of the inn's highest priced rooms.

We don't recommend the inn's least expensive rooms, which are small and offer no views.

THE SQUIRE TARBOX INN

Route 144
Wiscasset, ME
Telephone: (207) 882-7693

Eleven rooms, each with private bath; four rooms with woodburning fireplaces. Complimentary full breakfast served at tables for two in dining room. Dinner for two included in rates. No handicapped access. Smoking is not permitted. Two-night minimum required during holiday periods. Gratuity is added to total bill. Closed during winter. Moderate to deluxe.

Getting There
From Route 1, seven miles north of Bath, drive south on Route 144 for eight and a half miles to inn on right.

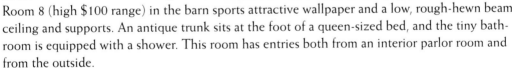

THE SQUIRE TARBOX INN

Wiscasset

One of the most unusual properties we've visited in New England, the Squire Tarbox Inn is a combination working goat dairy and country inn. Consequently, this property should have special appeal to couples who enjoy animals (not to mention cheese) and a casual country experience.

A mix of buildings that has evolved eclectically since the mid-1700s, the inn offers guests a range of overnight experiences, from small, countrified rooms to larger, more traditional bed-and-breakfast-style accommodations with fireplaces.

The inn's two-hundred-year-old lower dining room, with its barn-wood walls and ceiling and a view of Squam Creek, is particularly appealing. Also popular among guests is the well-tended barn where two wooden rope swings invite quiet time together. Dinner for two is included in the room rates, and various cheeses from the dairy are served to guests before the meal.

Rooms for Romance

In the property's original Federal-style home, Room 1 (low $200 range) is a nicely windowed front-facing corner with a king-sized bed, a love seat, and a working fireplace. The dark wood floor is covered with a braided rug. In the same price range on the second floor is the king-bedded Room 3.

Most honeymooners request rooms in the more rustic barn building. Room 8 (high $100 range) in the barn sports attractive wallpaper and a low, rough-hewn beam ceiling and supports. An antique trunk sits at the foot of a queen-sized bed, and the tiny bathroom is equipped with a shower. This room has entries both from an interior parlor room and from the outside.

We also liked Room 11 (high $100 range), a cathedral-ceilinged hideaway on the top level of the adjacent carriage barn building.

We found a few of the smaller accommodations in the barn buildings with low ceilings and tiny bathrooms to be somewhat confining.

FIVE GABLES INN

Murray Hill Road
East Boothbay, ME 04544
Telephone: (207) 633-4551 or
toll-free: (800) 451-5048

Sixteen rooms, each with private bath; five with
woodburning fireplaces. Complimentary full buffet
breakfast served at tables for two or in your room. No
handicapped access. Smoking is not permitted. Two-
night minimum stay during the month of August and
during holiday periods. Closed November through
mid-May. Moderate to expensive.

Getting There
From the Maine Turnpike (Interstate 95), take exit 22
and follow Route 1 to Route 27 south. Take Route 96
through East Boothbay. Turn right at blinking light
on Murray Hill Road and follow a half-mile to inn
on right.

FIVE GABLES INN
East Boothbay

$\mathscr{A}$ century ago, wealthy northeasterners escaped the muggy summers by visiting the more hospitable climes of coastal Maine. Of the numerous seasonal hotels that once catered to those vacationers along the mid coast, Five Gables Inn is the sole survivor. Don't expect a sagging relic, however. From the outside to the interior spaces, this crisp, stately hostelry looks like it could have been built yesterday.

Taking its name from the prominent windowed gables along its front, Five Gables Inn sits on a sloping lawn overlooking Linekin Bay and East Boothbay, a quiet shipbuilding village. Once a twenty-two-room hotel, the structure underwent a tasteful remodeling a few years ago that reduced the number of rooms to sixteen. Furnishings are traditional and the rooms are carpeted.

Rooms for Romance

Our most highly recommended room and the inn's most popular is Room 14 (mid $100 range), where two wing chairs flank a fireplace. There are two windows offering beautiful views of the bay and a king-sized brass-and-iron bed. The skylit bathroom has a shower stall.

Room 11 (around $100) is a nice gabled, third-floor corner hideaway that's furnished with a queen-size bed. We also recommend rooms 5 and 10 (low $100 range), two second-floor corners with queen-sized beds and bay views. Room 5 has a brick fireplace. Rooms 6 and 7 also have fireplaces.

Some of the inn's rooms, including rooms 2, 12, and 15, are a bit too small for our tastes, and the rooms on the first floor face either the back of the property, lacking a view, or a common front porch, lacking complete privacy if your windows are open.

THE INN AT HARBOR HEAD

41 Pier Road

Kennebunkport, ME 04046

Telephone: (207) 967-5564

Five rooms, each with private bath. Complimentary full breakfast served at a communal table or in your room. No handicapped access. Smoking is not permitted. Two-night minimum stay required. Closed late December through early January. Expensive to deluxe.

Getting There

From the Maine Turnpike (Interstate 95), take exit 3 and follow Route 35/9A south to Kennebunkport. Turn left at the intersection of routes 9 and 35, cross the bridge and follow Route 9 east through Dock Square. Turn right at top of hill and left at the Cape Porpoise signs. Follow Route 9 past the market and hardware store. Follow past the Wayfarer Restaurant and around the head of the cove to inn on right.

THE INN AT HARBOR HEAD

Kennebunkport

After touring the best of Kennebunkport's impressive collection of romantic inns and small hotels, we decided to bypass the more obvious choices and feature a couple of gems off the beaten track.

It took us two visits to Kennebunkport to discover the Inn at Harbor Head, which boasts an idyllic setting along the glassy waters of Cape Porpoise Harbor. Although only a three-minute car ride away, the bustling village of Kennebunkport might as well be a hundred miles away. The inn is on a quiet residential street, and the postcard view of the harbor and the lobster boats is a treat.

Operated by seasoned innkeepers David and Joan Sutter, the hundred-year-old shingled home

has been lovingly and elegantly converted into a cozy romantic retreat. Murals and other artistic treatments by Joan adorn each of the guest room walls.

Rooms for Romance

You'll be treated to a fine harbor view through the French doors of the Garden Room (upper $100 range), a small first-floor accommodation that features a Japanese theme. Joan's favorite room, Garden, holds a queen-sized four-poster bed with a harbor view, and a tiny bathroom with a shower stall. There's also a private water-view patio.

Also on the first floor is the Greenery (upper $100 range), formerly a Florida room. Although you won't see the water from this green-paneled room, you can soak in the warm water of the rose-colored spa tub for two in the beautiful mirrored and green-tiled bathroom.

In the second-floor Ocean Room (mid $100 range), a handsome pineapple-post bed is placed diagonally near a wicker love seat. This room offers a water view during the winter months when the leaves are off the trees.

Our favorite room is the Summer Suite (low $200 range), accessed by a private stairway from the library. Five windows boast a grand water vista, and the spacious room is furnished with a wicker chaise and love seat and a king-sized bed with a matching wicker headboard. The room also contains the inn's most sumptuous bathroom, a cathedral-ceilinged retreat that holds a step-up ocean-view spa tub for two, a marble vanity, and a bidet.

Another fine romantic choice is the Harbor Suite (low $200 range), whose sitting room is decorated with an expansive wall mural featuring a harbor scene. A queen-sized cherry tester bed and a comfy chaise are placed near a gas fireplace. The tiny tiled bathroom has a shower. Warm-weather visitors will savor the harbor view from this suite's private balcony.

BUFFLEHEAD COVE INN

Route 35
Kennebunkport, ME 04046
Telephone: (207) 967-3879

Six rooms, each with private bath; two with gas
fireplaces. Complimentary full breakfast served at
a communal table or in your room. No handicapped
access. Smoking is not permitted. Two-night minimum stay required during weekends and holiday
periods. Moderate to expensive.

Getting There
From the Maine Turnpike (Interstate 95), take exit 3
and follow Route 35/9A south to Kennebunkport. At
the intersection of routes 1 and 35, continue on Route
35 for three miles. Watch on right for realty office
sign and turn left on unmarked drive just beyond.
Follow to inn at end of drive.

BUFFLEHEAD COVE INN

Kennebunkport

As we made our way along the unmarked gravel drive from Highway 35 and caught our first glimpse of Bufflehead Cove Inn, it was as if we had discovered a pirate's map to hidden treasure. After snuggling into one of New England's most romantic rooms, we considered keeping this sensual secret to ourselves.

It's not without selfish reservation that we share with readers this memory-making discovery, which ranks as the definitive example of a romantic getaway.

An attractive, three-story, gray-shingled home with white trim, the inn overlooks the serene Kennebunk River, whose gentle waters rise and fall with the Atlantic tides. Former President Bush, whose summer compound is nearby, is among the local fishermen who troll the shallow waters here.

The inn is operated by Jim and Harriet Gott, southern Maine natives who generously share their travel tips with guests.

Rooms for Romance

The cozy, covered balcony on the second floor belongs to the Balcony Room (mid $100 range), furnished with a queen-sized brass bed, a wicker chaise, and a water-view window seat. The walls are hand-painted and sponge-treated, and the small bathroom has a tiled shower stall.

Next door, the River Room (low $100 range) holds a queen-sized brass and black-iron bed set at an angle. A private little balcony has a water view.

The Teal Room (around $100), the inn's smallest, has a double-sized brass bed and features wall paintings. The bathroom has a shower stall; the marble sink is in the bedroom. The pretty Garden Studio, accessed privately at the rear of the inn, is the only room without a water view.

The room in which we stayed, Hideaway (upper $100), was a heavenly cottage-like suite connected to the inn by one wall. Carpeted in wool and exquisitely decorated with Mexican art, a bookshelf, and plants, the spacious suite consisted of a sleeping area with a king-sized bed and a sitting area with a couch and a love seat. The two environments were separated by a custom-tiled, two-sided gas fireplace. Windows on three sides of the suite offer views of the adjacent woods, gardens, and river.

Hideaway's luxurious bathroom, the size of an average guestroom, boasted a deep corner-mounted spa tub for two under a skylight, a separate glass shower stall, and beautiful custom tile. A brass candelabrum at the edge of the tub added a crowning romantic touch.

Although a few of the inn's rooms are small, there are lots of enchanting outdoor places, including boats, a hammock, a river-and-village-view deck, and Adirondack-style tables and chairs.

VERMONT

DAYTIME DIVERSIONS

The New England Maple Museum and Maple Market, the largest establishment of its kind in the world, is located on Route 7 in Rutland, near our destinations in Chittenden and Woodstock. Rutland is also home to a Norman Rockwell museum.

Locally made gourmet goodies, clothing, and products are sold at the Stowe Foliage Crafts Fair, usually held the last week of September in Stowe.

Chittenden, Woodstock, and Ludlow are within easy reach of the Killington, Bromley, and Pico ski areas.

Vermont's oldest professional theater is located in Weston, between Grafton and Ludlow.

Last but not least, Ben and Jerry's Ice Cream Factory, open for tours and tasting, is located on Route 100, just north of Waitsfield in Waterbury.

TABLES FOR TWO

T. J. Buckley's, 132 Elliott Street, Brattleboro
  (near West Chesterfield, NH)
Hemingways, Route 4 near Killington
The Governor's Inn and the Old Tavern, both of
  which are described in this section, have their
  own highly rated dining rooms.
Four Columns Inn, Newfane
Chantecleer, Route 7A, Manchester
Mistral's, Route 11/30, Manchester Center
The Prince and the Pauper, 24 Elm Street,
  Woodstock

RABBIT HILL INN

Route 18 and Pucker Street
Lower Waterford, VT 05848
Telephone: (802) 748-5168 or
toll-free: (800) 762-8669

Twenty rooms, each with private bath; twelve with
fireplaces; five with tubs for two. Amenities include
in-room cassette players (with tapes) and coffee-
makers (with coffee). Complimentary full breakfast
served at tables for two or in your room. Swimming
pond and restaurant. Handicapped access. Smoking is
not permitted. Two-night minimum stay required during weekends for some rooms; two- to three-night
minimum during holiday periods. Rates include a
four-course dinner for two. Closed during April and
first two weeks of November. Expensive to deluxe.

Getting There
Lower Waterford is located near the junction of inter-
states 91 and 93. From Interstate 91, take exit 19 to
Interstate 93 south. Take exit 1 and turn right onto
Route 18 south. Drive seven miles to inn on right. From
northbound Interstate 93, take exit 44 and turn left
onto Route 18 north. Drive two miles to inn on left.

RABBIT HILL INN

Lower Waterford

*I*n our travels, we've met charming innkeepers who, despite an inferior property, still manage to send guests away with smiles. We've also visited splendid inns that were, unfortunately, run by innkeepers lacking in interpersonal skills. Only on rare occasions it seems do we experience the magic that's created when a first-class property is presided over by excellent hosts. Rabbit Hill Inn, operated by John and Maureen Magee, is one of those special places.

Set near the New Hampshire border less than an hour's drive from Canada, Rabbit Hill is our northernmost Vermont destination. But the distance from New England's major metropolitan areas only adds to the inn's allure. We arrived road-weary on a chilly afternoon, but a friendly pub, glowing fires, and soft music quickly set a warm, inviting mood. Even though her guests were strangers a few hours before, Maureen mingled with her several dozen visitors like a good friend.

The inn spans two Federal-period buildings. The columned, three-story main house dates from the 1820s; the smaller wing was added about thirty years later as a ballroom. Each has been refurbished with loving care. All rates include a four-course dinner for two.

Rooms for Romance

Your hearts will flutter upon entering the Loft (mid $200 range), accessed via its own stairway. Created in the early 1990s, this spacious room is set under an eave and holds a king-sized canopied bed. A pretty couch faces a gas fireplace, and nearby an artful Palladian-crowned window grouping overlooks the backyard and a wooded area beyond. Polished pine floors are covered with hand-hooked rugs. There's also a private outdoor deck and a second sitting area set with two Boston rockers. Through a tiny step-up dressing area, you'll enter a large bathroom that holds a big white spa tub for two and a separate shower stall.

High on the third floor is the femininely styled Nest (mid $200 range). A queen-sized bed with a frilly white tulle canopy is placed near a gas fireplace sitting area with a comfortable love seat of wicker and mahogany. In an adjacent dressing area, a cushioned wicker chaise and a wicker dressing table sit on a black-and-white checkerboard floor. A door here leads to your private sun deck. The bathroom holds a raised spa tub for two and a separate shower.

Make your reservation early for the Tavern's Secret (mid $200 range), a popular room with a king-sized canopied bed, a gas fireplace, colonial reproduction furnishings, and a built-in bookcase. We agreed not to reveal this room's ultra-romantic "secret," but you'll be pleasantly surprised.

THE INN AT THE
ROUND BARN FARM

East Warren Road
Waitsfield, VT 05673
Telephone: (802) 496-2276

Eleven rooms, each with private bath; four with gas
fireplaces. Complimentary full breakfast served in
dining room at tables of four, six, and eight. Swimming
pool. No handicapped access. Smoking is not permitted. Two-night minimum stay required during weekends; three-night minimum during holiday periods.
Moderate to expensive.

Getting There
From northbound Interstate 89, take exit 9 and follow
south to Middlesex and onto Route 100B. Follow to
Route 100 and drive south to Waitsfield. Turn left
on Bridge Street, pass over covered bridge, and bear
right at the fork onto East Warren Road. Follow one
mile to inn on left.

THE INN AT THE ROUND BARN FARM

Waitsfield

*N*ew England travelers who make a day trip to that famous Waterbury, Vermont, ice cream factory and then drive straight home are savoring only part of the treat. After a tour and taste, in-the-know couples head south just a few miles to a sumptuous hideaway that is to romantic inns what Ben and Jerry's is to gourmet ice cream.

The distinctive, twelve-sided shaker barn—one of just a few left in Vermont—is the establishment's signature structure, but it's what's inside the adjacent buildings that lures lovers to the Inn at the Round Barn Farm.

Rooms for Romance

The Joslin Room (mid $100 range), for example, sports walls painted a deep seductive cranberry. The king-size bed is covered with a canopy and the bathroom is outfitted with a spa tub that, alas, is big enough for only one.

On the second floor, the Jones Room (around $100) is a tiny but cozy room set under a sloping ceiling with exposed rustic beams. There's a romantic mountain and garden view from the double antique spool bed through a floor-mounted "belly" window. The bathroom holds a shower stall.

Guests will likely be quite satisfied with the aforementioned guest rooms, but we must admit to being smitten with four unbelievably romantic chambers that occupy what was originally the hayloft of an attached barn structure. The Sherman, Dana, English, and Richardson rooms (mid to high $100 range) will take your breath away. But reserve well in advance; these rooms are coveted.

In our opinion, the most romantic room in the house is Richardson, a very fresh and spacious hideaway with a row of floor-mounted mountain-view windows and a skylight. In addition to a lovely gas fireplace and a partially canopied king-sized bed, there's a cushy chaise and a love seat for cuddling. The bright step-down bath area holds a long spa tub for two set in a wooden frame and placed under windows with a pretty view. There's also a glass-enclosed shower stall.

Next door is the cathedral-ceilinged English Room. This impressive room has a king-sized bed and a sitting area furnished with a love seat set before a gas fireplace. The windows afford soothing views of the surrounding hills, and the bathroom has a large steam shower for two.

The equally tasteful Sherman and Dana rooms also boast gas fireplaces, romantic vistas, and steam showers for two.

The twin-bedded Bates Room on the first floor is situated a bit too close to the dining room for those who value privacy. The Terrace Room sits below ground next to a game room that's equipped with a pool table, an organ, and couches and chairs. A sixty-foot-long lap swimming pool runs through the historic round barn and into an adjacent greenhouse.

TULIP TREE INN

Chittenden Dam Road
Chittenden, VT 05737
Telephone: (802) 483-6213

Eight rooms, each with private bath. Rates include full dinner and breakfast served in a communal dining room. Complimentary refreshments served every evening. Smoking is not permitted. Two-night minimum stay required during weekends; two- to three-night minimum required during holiday periods. Expensive to deluxe.

Getting There
From northbound Route 7 just north of Rutland, pass the red brick power station (on your left) and turn right at the Y in the road at the country store. Follow road for approximately six miles. Just past the fire station, drive straight for a half-mile to inn on the left. For more detailed driving instructions from New York or Boston, request a map when making your reservation.

TULIP TREE INN

Chittenden

*S*ome traveling romantics we know seek out only those getaway destinations that allow them to disappear immediately into the woodwork and savor each other's exclusive company. For these folks, the "do not disturb" sign is always out, and breakfast arrives at their door on a tray.

For other couples, the romance of the road includes a chance to mingle with innkeepers and share a meal or conversation with fellow sojourners before retiring to a private guest room.

Those who find the latter experience appealing will savor every moment of a visit to Tulip Tree Inn, a delightful retreat hidden away in the Green Mountains of central Vermont.

Painted a soothing green and sporting white shutters and an inviting front porch, the structure was built more than 150 years ago as a farmhouse, and later was acquired by a colleague of Thomas Edison. Edison and Henry Ford are among the luminaries who have spent a night or two here. In the mid-1980s, the property was purchased by Ed and Rosemary McDowell, New Yorkers who traded successful city professions for life in the country as Tulip Tree's hosts.

The inn is located off the beaten path several miles from the closest town, but guests needn't worry about hopping in the car to search for a suitable restaurant. Both dinner and breakfast are included in Tulip Tree's rates, which start in the mid to upper $100 range per couple.

Before dinner, Ed summons guests by bell to the den for refreshments and conversation. Multicourse dinners, created by Rosemary, are taken at assigned tables in an intimate dining room. Wine is available from Ed's cellar, which has won several awards. A full breakfast is served here each morning at an appointed time.

Rooms for Romance

The most romantic room in the house is Room 4 (around $200), windowed on three sides and offering views of the trees. The room has pine flooring and is equipped with a raised, queen-sized four-poster bed. Although there's only one cushy chair, you'll be able to relax together in the spa tub set in a polished wood frame in the middle of the bathroom. The wallpapered bathroom also contains double sinks.

Room 3, a front-facing corner, holds a queen-sized bed and two wing chairs. The bathroom here is likewise fitted with a spa tub for two.

Located less than twenty miles from Killington, the inn is a popular destination among Vermont ski enthusiasts. During warmer months, the romantic sounds of an adjacent brook waft through open windows of the inn's front-facing rooms.

THE JACKSON HOUSE

37 Route 4 West
Woodstock, VT 05091
Telephone: (802) 457-2065

Twelve rooms, each with private bath. Complimentary full breakfast served only at a large communal table. Complimentary libations and hors d'oeuvres buffet served every evening. Swimming pond. No handicapped access. Smoking is not permitted. Two-night minimum stay required during weekends and holiday periods. Moderate to deluxe.

Getting There
From Boston (153 miles), follow Interstate 93 north to Interstate 89, and north to Vermont. Exit at Route 4 and follow through Woodstock and another mile and a half to inn on right.

THE JACKSON HOUSE

Woodstock

*F*rom the road, the historic farmhouse may appear as just another example of a grandmotherly quaint, bed-and-breakfast inn. But most grandmas could only dream of living like this; the Jackson House is one of the most exquisite inns we've discovered anywhere in New England.

This luxurious property represents more than a decade of careful and deliberate nurturing by friendly innkeepers Jack Foster and Bruce McIlveen. The two have created a dozen delightfully distinctive rooms whose captivating environs complement this particularly enchanting part of Vermont. Your room for the night might hold bronze statuary, silk wall coverings, French crystal, or Chinese porcelain. Many guest chambers have views of the inn's rambling backyard.

Rooms for Romance

The inn's most indulgent accommodation is Regency (low to mid $200 range), a huge third-floor suite with a living room, a dining room, a bedroom, a den, and a kitchen. The sleeping chamber contains a queen-sized antique Brazilian canopied bed, and the cozy bath has a skylight and a shower stall.

Also at the high end is Francesca (high $100 range), a third-floor chamber that reportedly cost some thirty thousand dollars to decorate. Furnishings include a queen-sized cherry sleigh bed handsomely detailed with wicker and an upholstered sofa and wing-back chair. A private balcony overlooks the expansive backyard.

Nicholas I, although decorated with floral chintz and seafoam green carpeting, is similarly furnished and priced. It's also on the third floor.

Priced in the mid $100 range and a favorite among romantics, Cranberry features mauve-colored silk wall coverings, Oriental rugs, a queen-sized four-poster bed, and a veranda accessed via French doors.

On the second floor, the Miss Gloria Swanson Room (mid $100 range), which hosted the late screen star several decades ago, features a floor and furnishings made of bird's-eye maple, and a cheerfully bright floral design carried from wall and window coverings to the queen-sized bedspread.

The world-class grounds are a soul-stirring lovers' sanctuary. In addition to acres of lawn and trees, a formal English garden, and lots of places for private conversation, the inn's backyard boasts a swimming pond whose gleaming man-made beach is of crushed marble.

The inn has a Woodstock address, but the fabled village, a mile or so to the east, is not within walking distance.

KEDRON VALLEY INN

Route 106
South Woodstock, VT 05071
Telephone: (802) 457-1473

Twenty-seven rooms, each with private bath.
Complimentary full breakfast served in dining room
at tables for two. Swimming lake with two white-sand
beaches, restaurant. Handicapped access. Smoking
is allowed. Two-night minimum stay required during
weekends and holiday periods. Closed during April
and for ten days preceding Thanksgiving. Expensive.

Getting There
From Boston (153 miles), follow Interstate 93 north to
Interstate 89, and north to Vermont. Exit at Route 4
and follow west to Route 106 south. The inn is five
miles beyond Woodstock village on the right, just
past the Kedron Valley Inn stables.

KEDRON VALLEY INN

South Woodstock

After a quick self-guided tour of Kedron Valley Inn's pretty grounds, we opened the front door of the main building and walked right in, hoping to peek inside a room or two. Instead, we found ourselves in the middle of a wedding mass. Not much doubt about the romantic potential of this place.

The inn's buildings previously operated as a stagecoach stop, a hotel, a general store, a tavern, and a post office, but today this intriguing compound serves up romance in twenty-seven rooms adorned with antique heirloom quilts, hand stenciling, and canopy beds. Many rooms have bed-view fireplaces or wood stoves on raised hearths.

Operated by former Wall Street executives Max and Merrily Comins, Kedron (pronounced KEEdron) Valley Inn should appeal both to couples who appreciate country quiet as well as to those who prefer shopping and civilization. The shops of Woodstock are only five country miles away.

The inn also serves dinner, which is available for around $40 extra for the two of you.

Rooms for Romance

On the third floor of the main house, Room 17 (high $100 range) is a large, five-windowed fireplace suite with a separate sitting room equipped with a sleeper sofa. The bed chamber has a queen-sized canopied bed and the bathroom has a spa tub for two and double sinks. Decorated with light yellow floral wallpaper and carpeted in sea blue, the room also features two framed pillowcases embroidered by Merrily's aunt.

Room 2 (high $100 range) also has a fireplace, a queen-sized bed, and a wide, pine-plank floor covered with hooked rugs. This second-floor room has windows on two sides and holds an intriguing antique medicine bottle collection.

The six rooms in the comfortably rustic, single-level lodge building (mid $100 range) all have fireplaces and exposed log walls as well as hand stenciling and antique heirloom quilts displayed on the walls. The bathrooms are equipped with tub-and-shower combinations. The best of these, Room 37, is a corner room with a queen-sized canopy bed and a cozy streamside outdoor terrace.

In the adjacent Tavern building, which dates from 1822, Room 22 (high $100 range) boasts a three-sided fireplace on a raised hearth that can be savored from both the bed and the sitting area. This bright second-floor room is decorated with framed covers of women's magazines from the late 1800s. The bathroom holds a tub-and-shower combination and an antique oak shaving stand. A long private deck overlooks the inn's perennial gardens.

Another top choice in the Tavern is Room 19, which has a large fireplace, a queen-sized canopy bed, a sitting area with two craftsman-style chairs, and a walk-in, iron-doored safe that goes back to the days when the building served as a post office.

ANDRIE ROSE INN

13 Pleasant Street
Ludlow, VT 05149
Telephone: (802) 228-4846 or
toll-free: (800) 223-4846

Nineteen rooms, each with private bath; nine with gas fireplaces; twelve with tubs for two. Amenities include complimentary candies, nuts, fruit, liquid refreshments, and use of bicycles. Complimentary full breakfast (not included with certain suites) served in dining room at tables for two or delivered in a hamper to certain suites. Complimentary refreshments served every evening. Multicourse dinners (around $60 per couple) available on Saturday nights. Full bar. No handicapped access. Smoking is not permitted. Two-night minimum stay required during winter weekends and holiday periods. Moderate to deluxe.

Getting There

From northbound Interstate 91, exit at Route 103 (exit 6) in Rockingham, and follow Route 103 north to Ludlow where Route 103 becomes Main Street. Turn left on Depot Street and drive one block to inn on corner of Depot and Pleasant streets.

ANDRIE ROSE INN

Ludlow

Vermont skiers who remember Ms. Andrie Rose's Pleasant Street Guest Lodge wouldn't recognize the place since Jack and Ellen Fisher took over a few years ago and began waving their magic wand. What was once a small, homespun winter refuge in the shadow of Okemo Mountain is evolving into an enchanting estate whose newest guest rooms rank, in our opinion, as Vermont's most romantic.

Rooms for Romance

An 1820s-era farmhouse is at the heart of the Fishers' compound. The shingled and shuttered home, completely restored, contains ten guest rooms as well as the inn's public rooms.

Our two favorites in the main house are Skylight and Summit View (mid $100 range), set at the rear of the inn under the eaves on the second floor. Both have spa tubs for two. In Skylight, a queen-sized bed sits on rose-colored carpeting under an angled skylight. Summit View, which also features a skylight, is equipped with a queen-sized antique carved bed from which you'll be able to gaze at Okemo Mountain.

Three other romantic main house rooms are Country Lace, Country Roses, and Sunrise, each of which is equipped with a tiled and wainscotted oval spa tub for two. Sunrise is a small room equipped with a double bed. These hideaways carry rates in the low to mid $100 range.

Romantics who value privacy might find the first floor Village Way Room situated a bit too close to the public areas.

A higher level of luxury and romance is offered in the separate guesthouse behind the main house, in which four mouthwatering suites await. Each has a gas fireplace, a spa tub for two, a television, and a videocassette player.

Two single-bedroom suites (around $200) occupy the top floor. Outrage, the first, holds a couple of overstuffed and oversized chairs with ottomans whose upholstery matches the bed and window coverings. A gas fireplace flickers within sight of a king-sized, canopied iron bed. The exquisitely wallpapered and marbled bathroom holds a large whirlpool tub under a window and a separate marble shower.

Next door is Double Diamond, which features a blue and white color scheme and white wicker furnishings and a canopied queen-sized bed, also of wicker. It has similar luxury appointments.

The ground floor consists of a pair of elegant two-bedroom, one-and-a-half-bath suites with kitchens (mid $200 range), which might work for two couples traveling together.

The Fishers recently renovated another adjacent building to create five additional luxury suites (low $200 range) with onyx spa tubs for two placed in the bedrooms. These are also equipped with videocassette recorders, CD players, and refrigerators.

THE GOVERNOR'S INN

86 Main Street
Ludlow, VT 05149
Telephone: (802) 228-8830 or
toll-free: (800) 468-3766

Eight rooms, each with private bath; two with fireplaces. Rates include full breakfast, an afternoon tea,
and a six-course dinner for two. Full bar. No handicapped access. Smoking is not permitted. Two-night
minimum stay required during weekends; three-night
minimum during holiday periods. Deluxe.

Getting There
From northbound Interstate 91, exit at Route 103
(exit 6) in Rockingham, and follow Route 103 north
to Ludlow where Route 103 becomes Main Street.
Inn is on the left.

THE GOVERNOR'S INN

Ludlow

Vermont-bound travelers for whom a memorable romantic getaway must combine fine food and lodging under one roof will be hard pressed to top the Governor's Inn. At this venerable destination, meals are part of the tariff and part of the romantic experience.

The inn is a three-story home set along Main Street at the edge of Ludlow's downtown district. The dining room is on the first floor; guest rooms are located on the second and third levels.

Rooms for Romance

Most of the inn's guest rooms and bathrooms are comparatively small, but each room is decorated handsomely with European antiques and pretty wall coverings. One of our favorites is Room 5 (mid $200 range), a more spacious corner hideaway carpeted in deep green and furnished with a queen-sized burled antique bed with a matching armoire and dresser. The in-room sink sits behind an antique screen, and the small bathroom contains a tub-and-shower combination.

The side-facing Room 3 (around $200) features a bay window set with two antique chairs, and has a tiny bathroom with a shower stall. Facing front on the third floor is Room 7 (low $200 range), a more modern, rose-carpeted room with a queen-sized bed under a skylight.

We do not recommend Room 8, whose nonromantic bath is across the hall. Both rooms 6 and 8 have twin beds. Rooms 1, 3, and 4 contain queen-sized beds.

The Governor's Inn continues to earn wide recognition as one of Vermont's finest restaurants. Proprietors Charlie and Deedy Marble are graduates of L'Ecole du Moulin-Roger Verge, a respected cooking school near Cannes, France, and Deedy has been cited as one of Vermont's most outstanding and innovative chefs.

The innkeepers present their tempting meals at private tables set with silver, crystal, and the family's antique china. Dinner is not served on Tuesdays, and the dining room is open to nonguests on a fixed-price basis ($50 range per person). Rates noted above include dinner for two.

CORNUCOPIA OF DORSET

Route 30
Dorset, VT 05251
Telephone: (802) 867-5751

Five rooms, each with private bath; two with
fireplaces. Complimentary full breakfast served at
communal tables. No handicapped access. Smoking
is not permitted. Two-night minimum stay during
weekends; two- to three-night minimum during
holiday periods. Moderate to expensive.

Getting There
From Route 7 in Manchester Center, drive north on
Route 30 for six miles to inn on right, just south of
the Dorset village green.

CORNUCOPIA OF DORSET

Dorset

As much as we look forward to a visit to lovely Manchester, the stores, cars, and shopping hordes eventually produce a yearn for those sleepy romantic villages for which Vermont is so well known. Dorset, just six miles north of the outlet centers, is within a quick drive of Manchester, yet far enough away to possess a distinctly quiet atmosphere. It's also the site of Cornucopia of Dorset, a charming home base for southern Vermont wanderings.

Located along Route 30 within earshot of the village church chimes, the Colonial-style inn is operated by Bill and Linda Ley, who maintain the century-old property in pristine condition.

The inn offers but five rooms, but Bill and Linda have created many comfortable public spaces in the main house, providing couples with opportunities for added private relaxation. Breakfast, served at communal tables in a spacious dining room, is not available in your guest room. A tray with coffee or tea and fresh flowers is available before breakfast in the main house guest rooms.

Rooms for Romance

One of Vermont's coziest lovers' hideaways is the Owl's Head cottage. Offered for around $200 per night, this former carriage house is a freestanding shuttered jewel set at the rear of the property against tall trees. On ground level, a love seat and chair sit on soft pine floors before a

brick woodburning fireplace. Adjacent to the comfy seating area is a full kitchen. The bathroom has a tub-and-shower combination. French doors open to a private patio facing an expansive back lawn. Upstairs is a carpeted loft containing skylights, a queen-sized bed, and an antique dresser and cradle.

The main house contains four guest rooms. The Scallop (mid $100 range) is a second-floor corner room with a brick woodburning fireplace, a queen-sized canopied bed, tall windows, and a spacious and sunny bathroom holding a tub-and-shower combination.

Our other favorite, Green Peak (low to mid $100 range), occupies a second-floor corner and is equipped with a queen-sized pencil-post bed and a large bathroom. A picture window affords pretty views of the backyard with its lawn, trees, and gardens.

Dorset Hill (low to mid $100 range) has a king-sized bed that can convert to two twins, and a small step-up bath with a shower stall. Mother Myrick (low $100 range) is a smaller, king-bedded room with a bathroom containing double sinks.

THE VILLAGE COUNTRY INN

Historic Route 7A
Manchester Village, VT 05254
Telephone: (802) 362-1792 or
toll-free: (800) 370-0300

Thirty-one rooms, each with private bath. Full breakfast and four-course dinner for two included in rate.
Meals are served in the inn's restaurant. No handicapped access. Smoking is allowed in the tavern only.
Two-night minimum stay required during weekends;
two- and three-night minimum during holiday periods.
Moderate to deluxe.

Getting There
From northbound Interstate 91, exit at Route 30 in
Brattleboro, VT, and follow north to intersection
with Route 11; turn left. Follow Route 11/30 west
for one and a half miles past Route 7 to Manchester.
Turn left at the blinking light on Route 7A and follow
to inn on right.

THE VILLAGE COUNTRY INN

Manchester Village

Whether its long roofline is glistening under a fresh dusting of snow, its fine porch is sprinkled with crisp new-fallen leaves, or its rear gardens shimmer in summer sunlight, the Village Country Inn possesses all the ingredients for casting one of New England's most romantic spells.

One of the gracious vintage edifices that contributes to Manchester Village's famous charm, the inn has been a part of the community for generations. And though it's a village landmark, the Village Country Inn doesn't simply offer enchanting curb appeal. Innkeepers Anne and Jay Degen, who have owned the inn since the mid-1980s, have created romantic interior spaces that weren't available to visitors in the old days.

Over the past decade or so, the couple has removed walls to enlarge rooms, infused guest chambers with pretty wall and window coverings, and improved outdoor living spaces.

Rooms for Romance

Rooms here are grouped as either standard or "larger special accommodations." We recommend the latter group, whose rates, including a breakfast and a four-course meal for two, range from the mid $100 range to just over $200 per night. Standard rooms, which have small private bathrooms, are offered in the mid $100 range, including breakfast and dinner. Some of these rooms have double beds.

In the larger special category, there are three types of rooms to choose from: "garden rooms," "large luxury rooms," and "suites." Garden rooms on the ground floor have private outdoor entrances, king- or queen-sized canopy beds, and televisions.

The large luxury rooms, sprinkled about the second and third floors, have king-sized canopied beds or queen-sized beds, some of which have canopies. The front-facing Room 106, for example, has a rose color scheme and contains a queen-sized iron bed with lace canopy. A love seat sits at the foot of the bed. The spacious carpeted bathroom has a rounded glass shower and a small old-fashioned tub on a tiled pedestal.

Among the inn's suites is Room 221 on the third floor overlooking the gardens, the gazebo, and the swimming pool. Situated within earshot of a gentle fountain, the large bedroom is illuminated by four windows. The king-sized bed features a pattern shared by a nearby chaise longue. A bathroom with a pedestal tub and a round shower separates the bedroom from a corner sitting room with wicker furnishings.

Since the inn faces the village's main thoroughfare, we recommend the side- or rear-facing rooms to those bothered by traffic noise.

1811 HOUSE

Route 7A

Manchester Village, VT

Telephone: (802) 362-1811 or

toll-free: (800) 432-1811

Fourteen rooms, each with private bath; six rooms with fireplaces. Complimentary full breakfast served at communal tables and tables for two. No handicapped access. Smoking is allowed in the pub only. Two-night minimum stay required during weekends; two- and three-night minimum during holiday periods. Moderate to expensive.

Getting There

From northbound Interstate 91, exit at Route 30 in Brattleboro, VT, and follow north to intersection with Route 11; turn left. Follow Route 11/30 west for one and a half miles past Route 7 to Manchester. Turn left at the blinking light on Route 7A and follow for one mile to inn on left.

1 8 1 1   H O U S E

Manchester Village

$\mathcal{S}$et on seven-plus lush acres in the shadow of a spired church, 1811 House is our top choice for a Manchester Village romantic rendezvous.

Its name suggests a nineteenth-century vintage, but the structure, one of the community's oldest, was actually built in the 1770s. It was converted from a home to an inn in 1811 and has

welcomed guests ever since, except for a time when it served as the home of Mary Lincoln Isham, granddaughter of Abraham Lincoln.

The inn boasts multiple antique-furnished public rooms, two of which have fireplaces, and there's a basement recreation room with Ping-Pong and billiard tables. A small English-style pub (called a snug) with a shiny wood bar is warmed by yet another fireplace. Oriental rugs are placed throughout the inn.

Rooms for Romance

In addition to the handsome Federal-style home, the property has a separate cottage containing three rooms. One of these, the cozy second-floor Mary Olson Room (around $200), is set under a wall-papered sloping ceiling and features a fireplace and two leather chairs. Most of the inn's rooms lack couches or love seats but have matching chairs.

Also in the cottage is the Lang Room (around $200), a romantic lamp-lit corner with several tall windows, a brick and wood-paneled fireplace, and a king-sized bed with a fishnet canopy.

In the main house, the handsome Robinson Room (around $200) on the second floor is the fall favorite because of its beautiful view. From your private balcony you can see across the length of the back lawn and gardens, over a pond and golf course, and to the distant Green Mountains. The room has a king-sized canopied bed and a bathroom with a clawfoot tub enclosed in marble.

In the Mary Lincoln Isham Room (around $200), two tall windows flank a wood-and-marble fireplace. A queen-sized canopied bed sits nearby.

Trimmed tastefully in reds, the elegant French Suite (around $200) has a king-sized canopied bed with a woodburning fireplace near its foot. A separate sitting room holds a couch.

The smallish Hidden and Icy Palmer rooms both have double beds and run in the low $100 range.

INN ON COVERED BRIDGE GREEN

River Road at Covered Bridge Road

Arlington, VT 05250

Telephone: (802) 375-9489 or

toll-free: (800) 726-9480

Six rooms, each with private bath; three with gas fireplaces. Complimentary full breakfast served at a large communal table or in your room. Tennis court. No handicapped access. Smoking is not permitted. Two-night minimum stay required during holiday periods. Moderate to expensive.

Getting There

From Route 7, take Highway 313 west (exit 3) through Arlington. Continue on Highway 313 for four and a half miles. Turn left at the covered bridge over the river and follow lane to inn, just past the church.

INN ON COVERED BRIDGE GREEN

Arlington

The red covered bridge, the green, the little church, the old farmhouse . . . no wonder Norman Rockwell chose this tiny village as his home. And those qualities that inspired one of America's most beloved artists make the Inn on Covered Bridge Green one of Vermont's most romantic getaway destinations.

Home of the Rockwell family for about a dozen years during the 1940s and early 1950s, the compound is today operated by Ron and Anne Weber, who settled here after spending time in England and Scotland. The Webers' five acres, bordered by apple orchards and horse and dairy farms, are situated along the Battenkill River.

Rooms for Romance

You'll savor one of New England's most memorable romantic experiences in the Norman Rockwell Studio, the little red cottage in which the master created many paintings. Set at the rear of the property against green hills, it's a spacious and somewhat rustic retreat whose homespun downstairs great room boasts a fireplace, a couch, a large table and chairs set, a love seat, and a big picture window. Also on this level are a full kitchen, a bedroom with twin beds, and a bathroom with a shower.

The upstairs loft has been romantically converted to offer a bedroom with a queen-sized bed and a sunny bathroom overlooking a pretty backyard scene. Patio doors open onto your own private view deck. Visitors should note that the studio may be rented as two units during the busy fall season, with guests sharing the living room. We don't recommend this arrangement, and suggest that couples desiring a private romantic getaway book the entire studio (low $200 range) for their exclusive romantic use. This comfortable unit has a two-night minimum.

The nearby Corn Crib (high $100 range) is a rustic freestanding accommodation that combines a cozy downstairs carpeted sitting room and a loft under the eaves with a queen-sized bed.

In the main house, the best room is Bicentennial (high $100 range), a second-floor rear corner that was added recently. The wool-carpeted room has a queen-sized, canopied four-poster bed placed diagonally and facing a gas fireplace. Two wicker chairs sit under corner windows. The bathroom contains a single-sized spa tub.

Our other main house favorite is Spooners (mid $100 range), the front-facing second-floor room that served as the master bedroom during the Rockwells' time. Furnishings include a queen-sized four-poster bed and a love seat; the village green and covered bridge are visible through the windows. There's also a gas fireplace.

THE OLD TAVERN AT GRAFTON

Route 35 at Route 121
Grafton, VT 05146
Telephone: (802) 843-2231

Sixty-six rooms, all but two with private baths. Complimentary continental breakfast served in the inn's restaurant. Swimming pool, restaurant, and lounge. Limited handicapped access. Smoking is allowed. Two-night minimum stay required during holiday periods. Closed mid-March through mid-May. Moderate to deluxe.

Getting There
From Interstate 91, take exit 5 on Route 121, at Bellows Falls, VT. Drive northwest on Route 121 approximately twelve miles to inn at intersection of routes 121 and 35.

THE OLD TAVERN AT GRAFTON

Grafton

*S*tubborn is the word that aptly describes most everything and everybody in Grafton, a town that has yet to get in step with the rest of the country. It's a town that still whitewashes its picket fences, shingles its bridges, and collects dripping maple sap in buckets.

It's not that time forgot Grafton. It's just that Grafton forgot, or rather refuses, to wind the clock. About the only sign of the modern age is the occasional car that whizzes through the village.

Rooms for Romance

Don't expect shiny Italian marble, rich window treatments, or bubbling spa tubs. What you'll find here are cozy rooms with comfortable traditional furnishings, a beaded rug here and there, and an occasional canopied bed. There are no televisions or telephones. It's more charming than luxurious.

Rooms are located not only in the multi-storied and balconied main building, but throughout a variety of nearby village homes.

We spent a night in the main inn, which contains fourteen guest rooms. Those on the third floor (mid $100 range), offering a large bedroom and dressing area, are the best bets. Third-floor rooms 9, 11, 14, and 15 (mid $100 range) have queen-sized canopy beds.

Among traveling romantics, the most popular room in the main inn is Room 9 (mid $100 range), a third-floor corner that has a daybed and a sitting area furnished with two club-style chairs. The bathroom contains a tub-and-shower combination.

We don't recommend the second-floor rooms for a romantic getaway.

The Whitegates property, a restored old Grafton home that's now part of the Old Tavern enclave, has four bedrooms. We recommend only Room 1. This large upstairs unit has a bay window and a bathroom with two sinks.

Although it was occupied by happy honeymooners at the time of our visit, Hillside Cottage (high $100 range) overlooking the village has been described to us as a very romantic hideaway. The cottage has a bedroom and living room.

We were not impressed with rooms in Homestead, a house across the street from the main inn.

The Old Tavern and several other Grafton buildings are owned and operated by the nonprofit Windham Foundation, Vermont's largest foundation.

NEW HAMPSHIRE

DAYTIME DIVERSIONS

Lake Spofford, just north of Chesterfield Inn in West Chesterfield, has boats for rent. In the same region, you can hike in and around Pisgah Park or take a dip in two spring-fed swimming ponds. In the winter, you can ice skate under the stars on frozen ponds at Chesterfield Inn and the Notchland Inn.

Summer visitors to Tamworth Inn need only cross the street to catch a play at the historic Barnstormer's Summer Theatre, the oldest professional theater in the nation. There's also a summer playhouse in New London in the Sunapee area.

Tamworth and Snowville visitors have easy access to the outlet shops of North Conway.

The Bernerhof and the Notchland Inn are conveniently close to the myriad outdoor attractions of the White Mountains and Mount Washington valley.

Mount Sunapee, Pat's Peak, and King Ridge ski areas are within an easy drive of our Sunapee region destinations.

TABLES FOR TWO

The majority of our recommended New Hampshire properties have their own dining rooms. In addition to these, we recommend:

T. J. Buckley's, 132 Elliott Street, Brattleboro, VT (near West Chesterfield, NH)

Millstone, Main Street, New London

Inn at Thorn Hill, Thorn Hill Road, Jackson Village

Country Spirit, Route 114, Henniker

THE NOTCHLAND INN

Route 302
Harts Location, Bartlett, NH 03812
Telephone: (603) 374-6131 or
toll-free: (800) 866-6131

Eleven rooms, each with private bath and woodburning fireplace. Complimentary evening refreshments. Rates include dinner for two. Hot tub and restaurant. No handicapped access. Smoking is not permitted. Two-night minimum stay required during weekends; two- to three-night minimum during holiday periods. Expensive.

Getting There

From Interstate 93, take exit 35 and follow Route 3 to Route 302. Turn right on Route 302 and drive through White Mountain National Forest for 21 miles to inn on right.

THE NOTCHLAND INN

Bartlett

A roaring waterfall, long lazy moments of warming sun, a brief mountain drizzle during which a family of moose appeared along the roadside, miles of sweeping ridges ablaze in autumn color . . . by the time we reached the heart of White Mountain National Forest, Mother Nature had dazzled us with four seasons' worth of magic. Then we rounded a bend at Harts Location and were greeted by a vivid rainbow arcing over the granite façade of the Notchland Inn. "Do you suppose all the guests get this kind of red carpet treatment?" my partner wondered.

We can't guarantee a rainbow, but visitors can count on spectacular scenery every day of the year and consistent hospitality at one of New Hampshire's most romantic inns.

The Notchland Inn is a handsome, eclectically styled building whose steep roofline is accented with enchanting dormers and gables. The inn sits just off the highway on four hundred acres within a rugged White Mountains notch. Mounts Crawford and Hope tower nearby.

During the warmer months, flower and herb gardens add splashes of color to the grounds. When snow arrives, the inn's pond freezes and guests are invited to skate under the moon. Throughout the year, a wood-fired hot tub awaits in an outdoor gazebo.

All rates include dinner for two.

Rooms for Romance

Room 1 (mid $100 range), a front-facing first-floor corner, has windows on three sides. Two wing chairs face a woodburning fireplace with a façade of jade-hued antique tile. The diagonally placed queen-sized bed has an antique Eastlake headboard. The tiny bathroom has a shower stall.

Room 2 (mid $100 range) has a queen-sized bed and an oak bureau with a mirror that reflects the fireplace and two blue wing chairs. French doors open to private porches.

On the second floor is the inn's king-bedded suite (high $100 range) with a sitting room equipped with a couch and chairs. Also on the second floor is Room 6 (mid $100 range), a king-bedded hideaway referred to as "The Spy Room." It takes its name from a World War II–era guest who spied on passing munitions trains from the tall windows.

For those who enjoy a bit of privacy, try the converted schoolhouse that sits at the rear of the property. This little dollhouse has two spacious accommodations, each offered in the high $100 range. The downstairs suite has a sitting room from which French doors open to a front-facing deck. The separate bedroom, which overlooks the pond, has a king-sized bed.

The inn's bathrooms, although all private, are small. Five have tub-and-shower combinations. The rest have shower stalls.

THE BERNERHOF

Route 302
Glen, NH 03838
Telephone: (603) 383-4414 or
toll-free: (800) 548-8007

Nine rooms, each with private bath; six with tubs for
two. Complimentary full breakfast served in inn's
restaurant. Restaurant and pub. No handicapped
access. Smoking is allowed in restaurant only. Two-
night minimum stay required during weekends and
holiday periods. Moderate to expensive.

Getting There
From Interstate 93, take exit 35 and follow Route 3 to
Route 302. Turn right on Route 302 and drive through
White Mountain National Forest to Glen. Inn is on
the left.

THE BERNERHOF

Glen

*I*n advance of our visit to Mount Washington valley, we read a magazine article about the Bernerhof's inn and restaurant in which one of the owners was quoted as saying, "Our purpose is food here. Our purpose is to be a restaurant." Despite this travelers' red flag, we decided to sample a room for a night. And while the dining room did seem to be the focal point, we were favorably impressed with the inn's comparatively bargain-priced romantic rooms with spa tubs for two.

Guest rooms are situated on the second and third levels of the gabled and turreted Victorian hotel. The inviting restaurant and pub occupy the ground floor.

Rooms for Romance

The hotel's most beguiling accommodation is Room 6 (mid $100 range), a huge suite that encompasses one entire side of the second floor. The bedroom (which unfortunately faces the highway) holds a king-sized brass and white-iron bed. A love seat sits in a corner bay. Through lace-covered French doors is another sitting room with a couch, a chair, and a small television. The bathroom boasts an elevated spa tub for two and stained-glass shutters that open over the tub onto the sitting room.

A less expensive but equally romantic choice is Room 3 (low $100 range), where a big rose-colored spa tub awaits in a mirrored corner near a queen-sized brass bed. Room 7 (mid $100 range), an attractive suite, also has a rose-colored spa for two as well as a sauna.

We settled in Room 4 (low $100 range), a spacious second-floor corner with a love seat positioned in the bay window and a king-sized brass bed covered with a wedding ring quilt. The room also held a huge oak armoire and a matching dressing table. The tiled bathroom held a luscious white spa tub for two with a shower extension. Stained-glass shutters opened from the tub onto the bedroom.

For a romantic getaway, we recommend only those rooms with spa tubs. We do not recommend rooms 2, 5, and 10.

For around $50 more per couple, guests can opt for the modified American plan, which includes dinner for two in the Bernerhof restaurant, highly rated for its innovative American and Swiss-Austrian cuisine. By the way, the Bernerhof is also the site of a well-known cooking school called A Taste of the Mountains. Also worth noting is the inn's convenient location near North Conway outlet stores and the Kancamagus Highway (Route 112).

Light sleepers should be advised that the inn's location along a busy highway means some road noise can be heard, especially during daytime traffic hours. However, if you're away skiing, shopping, or exploring during the day, you'll return to a quieter room with a cozy bed and a big soothing spa tub.

SNOWVILLAGE INN

Stuart Road
Snowville, NH 03849
Telephone toll free: (800) 447-4345

Nineteen rooms, each with private bath; five with
woodburning fireplaces. Full breakfast and dinner for
two included. Tennis court. No handicapped access.
Smoking not permitted. Two-night minimum stay
required during weekends; two- to three-night minimum during holiday periods. Moderate to expensive.

Getting There
From Interstate 95 at Portsmouth, exit north at
the Spaulding Turnpike and follow onto Route 16
north. Exit east on Route 25 at Ossipee and drive
to Effingham Falls. Turn left on Route 153 north and
follow for ten miles to Eaton and Crystal Lake. At
the Snowville/Brownfield sign, turn right and follow
past beach for one mile to Snowville. Turn right on
Fire Lane 37 (Stuart Road) and follow to inn.

SNOWVILLAGE INN

Snowville

istracted by the immediate roadside beauty during our drive up Foss Mountain to Snowville Inn, we were momentarily caught off guard by the magnificent view that awaited us at this charming turn-of-the-century former writers' retreat. From the inn's hillside perch, guests are greeted by a seemingly boundless vista that includes the enchanting Presidential Range. In fact, if you make the right reservation, you can wake up to one of New England's more memorable views.

A ten-acre compound under the new ownership of former New Yorkers Barbara and Kevin Flynn, the inn comprises eighteen rooms spread among three separate buildings: the Chimney House, the Carriage Barn, and the main inn, which also houses a large oak dining room with parquet floors where dinner and breakfast are served daily. The rates noted below include breakfast and dinner for two.

The inn is located approximately six miles from the North Conway outlet stores.

Rooms for Romance

In the main inn, our favorite is the queen-bedded Room 14, known as the Robert Frost Room (around $200). This former sun porch on the second floor has an entire wall of windows that overlook the White Mountains. The tiny bathroom has a shower stall.

Another great mountain view awaits in Room 9 (high $100 range), which has a queen-sized bed, knotty pine paneling, and a built-in desk. Unfortunately, the tiny bathroom here is purely functional.

While they don't offer mountain views, the rooms (low $200 range) in the Chimney House are among the inn's most romantic. All four of these more contemporary-style rooms have working brick fireplaces, queen-sized beds, pine floors and trim, and bathrooms that are a bit larger than those in the other buildings. One of these, Room 16, has a queen-sized canopy bed and offers a pretty view of the adjacent forest. The Chimney House rooms open onto a common room with a couch and a large brick fireplace.

In the more rustic Carriage Barn, the only accommodations we recommend for romantic getaways are rooms 5 and 6, although tall guests should be advised that Room 6 has a rather low knotty pine–beamed ceiling. We found the other rooms in this building to be rather small and confining and the bathrooms unappealing.

TAMWORTH INN

Main Street
Tamworth, NH 03886
Telephone: (603) 323-7721

Fifteen rooms, each with private bath. Complimentary full breakfast served at tables for two in the dining room or in your room. Rates include dinner for two. Swimming pool, restaurant, and pub. No handicapped access. Smoking is allowed only in the pub. Two-night minimum stay required during summer weekends; two- to three-night minimum during holiday periods. Moderate to expensive.

Getting There
From Interstate 95 at Portsmouth, exit north at the Spaulding Turnpike and follow onto Route 16 north. Continue past Lake Ossipee and turn left on Route 113. Follow into Tamworth to inn on left.

TAMWORTH INN

Tamworth

*D*on't come to sleepy Tamworth hoping for fancy whirlpool tubs or in-room fireplaces. You won't find them. Instead, you'll be welcomed by warm and friendly hospitality, comfortable country-fresh rooms, and a genuine, picture-perfect New England village.

The stately red-shuttered Victorian hotel, which has welcomed travelers since the mid-1800s, has fifteen rooms, a few of which have been expanded to suites with sitting rooms. The public areas are spacious and cozy, and there's also a rustic pub decorated with antique sleds. Just outside are a swimming pool and a fine yard with a gazebo. Meals are served either in the dining room or on the back porch that overlooks the lawn and the Swift River, which skirts the property. Rates include breakfast and dinner for two

The historic Barnstormer's Summer Theatre, the oldest professional theater in the nation, is just down the lane.

Rooms for Romance

Room 1, the inn's original bridal suite (mid $100 range), was visited in the early 1930s by an itinerant artist who painted murals on the wall in exchange for lodging. These are now framed out of the wallpaper. His work is also evident on the room's dresser. This room has a king-sized brass bed and faces front.

Among the favorites of romantic weekenders is Room 5 (low $100 range), which holds a king-sized brass and iron bed. The bathroom has a tub-and-shower combination.

Room 3 (low to mid $100 range) is a pretty corner suite with a queen-sized canopied bed and a sitting area furnished with a love seat. The small bathroom has a tub-and-shower combination. On the third floor is Room 29, another similarly priced suite with a king-sized canopied bed and a sitting area with two wing chairs. The tiny bathroom has a shower stall.

There are a few lower priced rooms with rates just over $100, including dinner for two; however, we decided these were a bit too small. Guests should be aware that the inn welcomes pets.

HOME HILL COUNTRY INN AND FRENCH RESTAURANT

River Road
Plainfield, NH 03781
Telephone: (603) 675-6165

Nine rooms, each with private bath. Complimentary
continental breakfast served at tables for two in the
dining room. Swimming pool, clay tennis court, and
six-hole golf course. No handicapped access. Smoking
is not permitted. Two-night minimum stay during
special weekends and holiday periods. Moderate to
expensive.

Getting There
From Interstate 89, take exit 20 and drive south on
Route 12A for three miles. Turn right on River Road
and drive three and a half miles to the inn's driveway
on right.

HOME HILL COUNTRY INN AND FRENCH RESTAURANT

Plainfield

*S*urrounded by peaceful woods, the nearest town miles behind us, it was easy to imagine our romantic selves transported to France, where hidden country inns like this lure the city-weary with fine food and comfortable accommodations. Our fantasy was further enhanced by easy conversation with and a wonderful dinner prepared by French innkeeper and chef Roger Nicolas,

who created the inn from a grand old Federal-style mansion. Prior to Nicolas's ownership, the home had passed through seven generations of the same family over a period of 150 years.

Painted white and shuttered in blue, Home Hill Country Inn stands in a clearing near the banks of the Connecticut River, just a few miles north of the longest covered bridge in America.

Rooms for Romance

In the main house, our favorite is the Master Bedroom Suite (mid $100 range), a high-ceilinged front corner room with a decorative fireplace and a queen-sized bed with a wood-and-cane headboard. In the bathroom is a small soaking tub for two that doubles as a shower.

The Blue Room (low to mid $100 range) is a nice room with a queen-sized brass bed and an antique love seat. However, the bath is small and the sink is doll-sized.

The Pine Room (low to mid $100 range) is nicely windowed with views of trees and the inn's new six-hole golf course. The bathroom has a small old-fashioned tub with a shower extension.

We don't recommend Isabelle's Room.

During our fall visit, we sampled Hillside (low to mid $100 range), one of three more contemporary-style rooms in the nicely renovated carriage house, whose exterior is pictured here. Hillside sits under the eaves on the second floor, a dormer window overlooking the golf course and forest beyond. The walls were delicately stenciled and the wood-framed windows were trimmed in blue. The queen-bedded room held a small table and chairs, but unfortunately lacked a place for the two of us to sit together. The modern bathroom held a pedestal sink and a tub-and-shower combination.

The Poolhouse (mid $100 range) is a remote structure that sits under tall trees at the edge of a forested ravine. Not available during winter months, this restored hideaway holds a sitting room with wicker furnishings, a separate bedroom with a double-sized bed, and a large bathroom with a tub-and-shower combination. The inn's swimming pool is just steps away.

During the wet season, we recommend a cozy room in the main house so as to avoid a walk through snow or rain to and from the dining room. We prefer the Carriage House rooms or the Poolhouse during nicer weather.

The above room rates include continental breakfast. Plan on spending around $100 or more for a nice dinner for two with wine served in the dining room of the main house.

THE ROSEWOOD COUNTRY INN

Pleasant View Road
Bradford, NH 03221
Telephone: (603) 938-5253

Seven rooms, each with private bath. Complimentary full breakfast served at tables for two. No handicapped access. Smoking is not permitted. Two-night minimum stay required during holiday periods. Moderate.

Getting There
From Interstate 89, exit at Route 202 and follow toward Keene. Take the Henniker/Bradford exit (Route 114) and follow for ten miles, then turn left at each of the next two traffic lights. At the end of the road, curve left and drive up the hill for nearly two miles. Turn right on Pleasant View Road and follow to inn, which is the third house on the right.

THE ROSEWOOD COUNTRY INN

Bradford

Because the rates of some of our most highly recommended rooms are beyond the reach of some couples, we occasionally hear from economically minded travelers who are looking for a romantic bargain. We found one in the Lake Sunapee region above the little town of Bradford.

Set a comfortable distance from neighbors and town activity, the three-story Rosewood Country Inn reminds us more of a large comfortable country home than of an inn that's been welcoming visitors since before the turn of the century. The guest book has been signed by such luminaries as Charlie Chaplin, Jack London, Lillian and Dorothy Gish, and Mary Pickford.

Well maintained and sporting dozens of rose-colored shutters, the inn is decorated with a mix of furnishings that range from antique to traditional. Hand stenciling is featured throughout.

Rooms for Romance

Our preferred room is the Bridal Suite, which occupies a bright turreted corner on the second floor. The seven-windowed room has a queen-sized bed over which grapevines and faux roses form a romantic canopy. A wicker love seat sits in the turret. The small bathroom holds a tub-and-shower combination. Offered at the time of our visit for less than $100, this room is one of New England's best bargains. Also, there's no minimum stay requirement, except during holidays.

With the exception of the large Bridal Suite, rooms here, while romantically cozy, are small. Larger people and those who are used to big beds should take note that most rooms contain double beds. Also, the private bathrooms are purely functional and there are no in-room couches or love seats for cozy snuggling.

If the Bridal Suite is unavailable, we recommend either Room 6 or Room 7, both of which are on the third floor. In Room 6, a pretty double-size canopied bed sits on a rose-colored rug over

hardwood floors. Tasteful stenciling graces the walls of Room 7, another double-bedded room that's a bit larger. These and all the inn's other rooms carry rates below $100.

Each morning, the Rosewood Country Inn departs from the predictable bed-and-breakfast experience by treating guests to a romantic three-course breakfast served in the dining room at candlelit tables for two on crystal place settings.

CHESTERFIELD INN

Route 9
West Chesterfield, NH 03466
Telephone: (603) 256-3211

Thirteen rooms, each with private bath; eight with fireplaces. Complimentary full breakfast served at tables for two in the inn's restaurant. Handicapped access. Smoking is not permitted in eleven of the rooms. Two-night minimum stay required during holiday periods. Moderate to expensive.

Getting There
From Interstate 91 in Vermont, take exit 3 north of Brattleboro and follow Route 9 west for two miles over Connecticut River to inn on left.

CHESTERFIELD INN

West Chesterfield

*C*ommanding a gentle hillside along a rural highway a couple of miles from the Connecticut River, Chesterfield Inn is difficult to categorize. It's not a country-home-turned-inn; it's not a motel; nor is it a typical hotel, although it has hotel-like interior hallways. It's an appealing century-old hybrid that evolved from diverse stints as a tavern, a farm, and a museum.

With generously sized, well-appointed rooms, interesting exposed beams, balconies, and fireplaces, we found the property very well suited to its newest incarnation as a romantic country inn and one of the region's best restaurants.

The community of West Chesterfield itself isn't on our list of New England's most romantic destinations, but the inn is definitely worthy of an overnight visit if your itinerary takes you past or near southwestern New Hampshire or southeastern Vermont.

Rooms for Romance

Guests may choose from rooms in the main inn building or four newer rooms in the Johanna Wetherby Guest House overlooking either a nearby meadow or an adjacent pond.

Room 17 (mid $100 range) in the main inn, our home for a night, was a bright corner with massive wooden trusses placed above a king-sized bed. Two wing chairs sat in a corner sitting

area, and French doors opened to our own small sunset balcony offering a view of the hills through trees. The large bathroom was equipped with a tub-and-shower combination,

Another of our favorites is Room 18 (mid $100 range) in the main inn, where weathered barn wood has been incorporated into the fireplace wall and beamed ceiling. This corner room has a king-sized bed, a large bathroom with a tub-and-shower combination, and a view of the Vermont hills.

There's an antique love seat in Room 12, which offers a view of the pond and hills. This ground-floor room has a king-sized bed and a small deck with chairs.

Room 11 faces the entry walkway and consequently isn't completely private unless the drapes are drawn. Room 10 (mid to upper $100 range), the honeymoon suite on the ground floor, has a spa tub for two and a fireplace. However, its front-facing view is also not completely private. Room 13 has two double beds.

In the guest cottage, rooms 21 and 24 (mid $100 range) are our favorites. Room 21 has a queen-sized four-poster bed, a fireplace, deep green carpet, and a spacious tiled bath with a tub-and-shower combination. A private patio overlooks the pond.

You'll have a meadow and hill view from Room 24, equipped with a queen-sized four-poster bed and a fireplace. French doors open to a private brick patio surrounded by a perennial garden.

MASSACHUSETTS

DAYTIME DIVERSIONS

Summer in the Berkshires means theater and music, and options range from the Stockbridge Cabaret and Tanglewood Music Festival in Lenox to the popular Berkshire Theatre Festival in Stockbridge. The Norman Rockwell Museum is on Main Street in Stockbridge.

The famous Salem Wax Museum, 288 Derby Street in Salem, is only a short distance from our Cape Ann destinations.

In Rockport, you can see the sights by taking a walking tour (ask your innkeeper for a map) or by catching a Cape Ann Tours trolley car. The village shops in Rockport will keep you busy for hours.

On Martha's Vineyard, the red and orange cliffs at Gay Head are among the most popular destinations among island combers. Bicycling is also big on the Vineyard, where cycle paths run along the ocean between Oak Bluffs and Edgartown. Ask your innkeeper for locations of rental shops and inspiring routes.

A multi-image production about life on Nantucket by island resident Cary Hazlegrove (who created the photos for this book) is shown daily during the summer months in the Methodist Church on Centre Street. Call (508) 228-3783.

TABLES FOR TWO

La Bruschetta, 1 Harris Street, West Stockbridge
Sweet Basil Grille, Routes 7 and 20, Lenox
Pellino's, 261 Washington Street, Marblehead
Christian's, Main Street, Chatham
Red Pheasant, Route 6A, Dennis
Le Grenier, Main Street, Vineyard Haven
Tisbury Inn Cafe, Main Street, Vineyard Haven
L'étoile at the Charlotte Inn, 27 South Summer
  Street, Edgartown

BLANTYRE

Blantyre Road

Lenox, MA 01240

Telephone: (413) 637-3556, May through October;
(413) 298-3806, November through April.

Twenty-three rooms, suites, and cottages, each
with private bath; six with woodburning fireplaces;
one with wood stove. Complimentary continental
breakfast served at tables for two or in your room.
Restaurant, heated swimming pool, sauna, spa,
tennis courts, and croquet lawns. Handicapped
access. Smoking is allowed. Two-night minimum
stay required during weekends and holiday periods.
Closed during winter. Deluxe.

Getting There

From the Massachusetts Turnpike (Interstate 90), take
Route 20 at Lee (exit 2) and drive west for three miles
to Blantyre on the right. Lee is approximately two
hours from Boston and just under three hours from
New York.

BLANTYRE

Lenox

A gated twenty-five-acre country estate, Blantyre is the most exclusive of our fifty romantic New England destinations. Travelers who enjoy formal elegance and being pampered in exquisite accommodations will feel quite comfortable in this magnificent Scottish-style manor.

Originally a private summer retreat, the turn-of-the-century property was restored by Senator John Fitzpatrick and his wife, Ann, during the 1980s and opened as an upscale inn.

The baronial public rooms of the main house are reminiscent of a royal palace. The priceless antique furnishings, museum-quality tapestries, ornately carved wooden ceilings and walls, and leaded glass windows are awe-inspiring.

Fixed-price meals (jacket and tie required) are served in a beautiful octagon-shaped dining room with fabric-covered walls.

Rooms for Romance

The eight guest rooms in the main house contain many of the same elegant trappings found in the public spaces. Our romantic favorite is the Laurel Suite (around $400), in which a queen-sized four poster bed is placed in a draped bay window. This beautifully papered room also has a woodburning fireplace and a sitting area with a couch and cushy chairs.

Least expensive are the Ribbon Room with a king-sized bed; the Bouquet Room with a queen-sized bed; and the Ashley Room, a small hideaway with a queen-sized bed and a sitting room. Each is available in the mid $200 range. The Blue Room (high $300 range) has two double beds.

We prefer the rhapsodic environs of the turreted main house, but Blantyre does offer other options that include a collection of somewhat less inspired rooms in a remote two-story carriage house and three cottages.

Fernbrook, on the second floor of the carriage house, is a romantic two-level room with a small balcony. The lower level is a large sitting room with a couch, a chair, and a table and chairs set; the loft, with a queen-sized bed, is accessed by an iron stairway. Carriage house rooms range from the mid $200 range to around $300.

Cottage Queen, with a queen-sized bed and bathroom with a shower, is Blantyre's least expensive accommodation, offered at the time of our visit in the high $100 range.

CHAMBÉRY INN

199 Main Street
Lee, MA 01238
Telephone: (413) 243-2221 or
toll-free: (800) 537-4321

Eight rooms, each with private bath; seven with gas
fireplaces. Complimentary continental breakfast
brought to your room. Restaurant next door provides
room service to inn guests. Handicapped access.
Smoking is not permitted. Two-night minimum stay
required during weekends. Moderate to expensive.

Getting There
From the Massachusetts Turnpike (Interstate 90), take
Route 20 at Lee (exit 2) and drive west for one mile
to inn on left. Lee is approximately two hours from
Boston and just under three hours from New York.

Old St. Mary's School
Built in 1885 as Berkshire
County's first Parochial
School. Slated for
demolition, was moved to
this site May 23, 1989
• by JOSEPH M. TOOLE •

CHAMBÉRY INN

Lee

*H*eading for the stairs to the guest rooms of this former schoolhouse, we were momentarily taken aback. In a tongue-in-cheek tribute to days past, signs reading "girls" and "boys" still hang over the two staircases. Apparently, relations between the genders weren't always as warm and cozy here as they are today.

If only the teaching nuns of old Saint Mary's School could see the place now. Romantic messages scrawled on in-room blackboards, fireplaces, king-sized canopied beds, intimate spa tubs . . . school was never like this!

Actually, the blackboards, his-and-hers stairways, creaky floors, and embossed ceilings are some of the few reminders of what was once the Berkshires' first parochial school. In addition to contemporary features like air conditioning, color televisions, and wall-to-wall carpeting, the building has a new location, having been moved one block from its original site before undergoing refurbishing in 1989. The new owners christened the inn after Chambéry, France, the native town of the Sisters of Saint Joseph who settled here in 1885 and built the school.

Rooms for Romance

Rooms at the Chambéry Inn are among the largest we've seen, some reaching 500 square feet. You'll either have a king-sized bed or two queens, with room to spare. Six rooms have thirteen-foot-high embossed ceilings and eight-foot-tall windows, all carefully preserved from the school days.

All but one of the rooms have gas fireplaces; each is equipped with a color television and telephone. Four suites have king-sized canopy beds. Bathrooms are modern and tiled, and feature spa tubs into which the two of you might be able to squeeze.

There are two rooms priced in the low $100 range on the lower level (the inn is set against a knoll), but we prefer those on the main and upper floors, which carry peak rates of around $200. Winter rates are considerably less expensive.

Room 301 is a third-floor front-facing corner with a love seat and two wing chairs, in addition to a gas fireplace. Next door, Room 302 is a rear-facing corner suite with similar furnishings.

By the way, guests are invited to contribute messages or doodles to the chalkboards that grace each room. And you won't be graded on spelling.

MERRELL TAVERN INN

1565 Pleasant Street
South Lee, MA 01260
Telephone: (413) 243-1794 or
toll-free: (800) 243-1794

Nine rooms, each with private bath. Complimentary
full breakfast served in dining room at tables for two.
Handicapped access. Smoking is not permitted.
Two-night minimum stay required during weekends;
three-night minimum during summer months and
holiday periods. Moderate.

Getting There
From the Massachusetts Turnpike (Interstate 90),
take exit 2 (Lee) and follow signs for Route 102 west
toward Stockbridge. Follow Route 102 for three miles
to inn on left.

MERRELL TAVERN INN

South Lee

When we learned in advance of our visit that Merrell Tavern Inn was celebrating its bicentennial, our first visions were of bedpans, candles, and drafty rooms. Instead, we were greeted by a stylishly enchanting environment with fully-equipped private bathrooms, queen-sized canopied beds, smart decor, romantic lighting, and innkeepers committed to a comfortable and romantic blend of old and new.

A national heirloom built around 1794, the building originally functioned as a residence but has served as a tavern and inn for many generations. Still in place are a number of antique fixtures, including what is believed to be the nation's only remaining birdcage-style bar, through which spirits and ales were undoubtedly liberally dispensed over the years. Fireplaces that warm the public and guest rooms are also original to the building, and many of the inn's antique furnishings date from the 1790s.

Rooms for Romance

We have favorites on each of the three floors. On the first level, Room 1 (mid $100 range), originally the inn's parlor, is among the larger rooms, and boasts a wood-burning fireplace and a queen-sized canopy bed.

On the second floor, rooms 2 and 9 (mid $100 range) also have fireplaces. Room 9 is a corner room with pine floors and a gold velour love seat.

Tastefully painted deep purple walls await behind the door of Room 7 (mid $100 range) on the third floor. This corner room is furnished with a queen-sized bed with a macramé canopy and handsome antiques. The wallpapered bathroom has a shower stall. We found rooms 5 and 10 (low $100 range) to be a bit small.

Room 6 (mid $100 range), our room for a night, was situated on the third floor, carved from space that originally served as a ballroom. Rose designs on the spread of the queen-sized bed were carried through to window hangings and the wallpaper border, as well as to the bed linens. The modern shower in our white tiled bathroom lacked sufficient water pressure, but such are the idiosyncrasies of older buildings, especially one built while George Washington was president.

YANKEE CLIPPER INN

96 Granite Street

Rockport, MA 01966

Telephone: (508) 546-3407 or

toll-free: (800) 545-3699

Twenty-six rooms, each with private bath. Complimentary full breakfast served in summer and fall; continental breakfast served in winter and spring; served in restaurant. Unheated salt water swimming pool. No handicapped access. Smoking is not permitted. Two-night minimum stay required during weekends; three-night minimum during holiday periods. Closed January and February. Moderate to deluxe.

Getting There

From Interstate 95, drive northwest on Route 128 to Cape Ann. In Gloucester, turn left on Route 127 and follow four miles to a five-corner intersection in Rockport. Make a sharp left turn (follow sign for Pigeon Cove) and follow for one and a half miles to inn's office on left.

YANKEE CLIPPER INN

Rockport

*I*f you were to ask a typical American traveler to name a romantic New England coastal getaway destination that's within a short drive of Boston, chances are the answer would be Cape Cod. Put the same question to a Bostonian in-the-know and the whispered response is more likely to be Cape Ann.

Long a favorite destination among Bay State residents, Rockport and Cape Ann's other enchanting towns have never quite achieved the mythical status of those on the world famous cape to the south. However, they remain some of New England's most shimmering seaside jewels.

Commanding a gentle ocean-view knoll at the rocky edge of the Atlantic, Yankee Clipper Inn represents the best of Cape Ann. It's conveniently close to the inviting shops of Rockport but is set in a quiet residential area of town. The inn has been owned by the same family for two generations.

The Yankee Clipper compound, which straddles a well-traveled street, includes three very different buildings. The oldest is the Bulfinch House, a 150-year-old Greek Revival home. On the ocean side of the street is the Inn, an eclectically designed seaside mansion set just yards from the surf. The inn's restaurant, common areas, and several guest rooms are located here. A stone path leads to the Quarterdeck, a three-story ocean-front structure built in the 1960s.

Rooms for Romance

At the time of our visit, innkeepers Barbara and Bob Ellis were in the midst of upgrading many of the rooms. We stayed in the freshly spruced-up room 37 (upper $100 range) on the ground floor of the Quarterdeck, which contained comfortable deep-cushioned wicker chairs and a king-sized bed. Through our large picture window, we watched the ocean turn from a sparkling late afternoon blue to a seductive dusky black. Our Quarterdeck favorites are those on the second and third floors, where you'll be able to savor the ocean view through open drapes without compromising your privacy.

In the Inn building, there are eight attractive guest rooms. John and Jacqueline Kennedy spent the night in Room 24 during a campaign trip in 1959. Offered in the low $200 range, this is a spacious corner suite with a king-sized bed, a comfy chaise, built-in bookshelves, and a private sun porch whose seven windows boast an expansive ocean view.

Rooms 27 and 31 (high $100 range) share a high outdoor sun deck, and Room 23 (low $200 range) has its own enclosed glass porch.

In the Bulfinch House, where more moderate prices prevail, we recommend only Room 16 (upper $100 range), an ocean-view stunner with a queen-sized canopy bed and a spa tub for two set in a mirrored corner of the room. A separate small bathroom has a shower stall.

HARBOR LIGHT INN

58 Washington Street
Marblehead, MA 01945
Telephone: (617) 631-2186

Twenty rooms, each with private bath; eleven have woodburning fireplaces; five have spa tubs for two. Complimentary continental breakfast served in dining room at communal table or in your room. Swimming pool. No handicapped access. Smoking is allowed in six guest rooms; not permitted in common areas. Two-night minimum stay required during weekends and holiday periods.

Getting There

From Interstate 95, follow Route 114 east to Salem-Marblehead, where it becomes Pleasant Street. Follow Pleasant Street to end and turn left onto Washington Street. Follow two blocks to inn on right. From Boston, follow Route 1A north to Route 129 east. In Marblehead, follow Atlantic Avenue and take the first right turn after filling station onto Washington Street. Follow one-quarter mile to inn on right. Parking is behind the inn.

HARBOR LIGHT INN

Marblehead

$\mathcal{M}$arblehead is less than twenty miles from the highrises of cosmopolitan Boston, but the roots of this historic village are still firmly planted in the eighteenth century. Among the intriguing old façades facing narrow Washington Street in the town's historic section are those of Harbor Light Inn, created through the union of two venerable homes constructed in the early 1700s.

Although the Harbor Light is our oldest romantic New England getaway destination, its age is quite deceiving. Sure, there are the requisite trappings of another time, such as fine wood, brass, and mason work, as well as the occasional creaky floorboard. But the inn's operators have taken great pains to provide contemporary comforts, like spa tubs for two in several rooms. There's even a swimming pool hidden in the rear courtyard.

Rooms for Romance

Room 22 (high $100 range) is the most popular, primarily because of the raised spa tub for two that sits surrounded by green plants under a skylight in a mirrored bathroom. The bedroom holds a queen-sized canopied bed and a working fireplace.

During the summer months, Room 4 (high $100 range) at the rear of the inn is a favorite because of its private outdoor deck. This room is furnished with a queen-sized four-poster bed, a love seat, and pine furnishings. The small bathroom holds a square spa tub for two.

Room 5 (high $100 range) is a remote front-facing corner on the first floor. In addition to a handsome, carved, queen-sized canopy bed, this room holds a window seat, two wing chairs, a fireplace, and a rug-covered oak floor. There's a spa tub for two set under a glass-block window in the bathroom.

Room 6 (upper $100 range), which faces the inn's rear courtyard, has a fireplace with an original bread oven. This room also has a spa tub for two.

All the guest rooms on the third floor have dark, rough-hewn, exposed beam ceilings. One of these, Room 32 (mid $100 range), is an attractive three-windowed corner with a small brick fireplace, bookshelves, and a queen-sized four-poster bed. The tiled bathroom has a tub-and-shower combination.

Smoking is allowed in a few of the romantic guest rooms here, so nonsmokers should be sure to request smoke-free accommodations.

WEDGEWOOD INN

83 Main Street (Route 6A)
Yarmouth Port, MA 02675
Telephone: (508) 362-5157 or (508) 362-9178

Six rooms, each with private bath; four with wood-burning fireplaces. Complimentary full breakfast served at tables for two or in your room. Complimentary tea served every afternoon. Handicapped access. Smoking is allowed in guest rooms but not in common rooms. No minimum stay requirements. Moderate to expensive.

Getting There
From eastbound Route 6 on Cape Cod, take exit 7 and turn right. Drive one mile to Route 6A and turn right. Inn is on the right.

WEDGEWOOD INN

Yarmouth Port

An elegantly shuttered façade, quilted and canopied beds, cozy fireplaces, gracious innkeepers, even a squeaky floorboard here and there. Yes, that romantic Cape Cod inn you've day-dreamed about really does exist.

We discovered these beguiling qualities at Wedgewood Inn, a six-bedroom bed-and-breakfast inn that stands among dozens of stately vintage charmers along Route 6A at the heart of historic Yarmouth Port.

Set on a grassy knoll surrounded by fine old trees, the meticulously restored structure was inspired by Greek Revival and Federal styles and is said to have been the town's first architecturally designed home. Built for a town attorney in 1812, the three-story home has operated as an inn since the early 1980s.

Our tour guide was innkeeper Milt Graham, a former New England Patriots offensive tackle whose towering presence belies his gentle nature. Milt shares innkeeping duties with his wife, Gerrie, who earlier worked as a professional dancer and school teacher.

Rooms for Romance

Guest rooms are outfitted with rich furnishings, including cherry wood pencil-post beds, cushy chairs, and attractive wall and window coverings. Some rooms have original wide-plank pumpkin-pine floors. There are no in-room telephones or televisions at the inn.

Rooms 1 and 2 (mid $100 range) on the first floor are first-class, all-season romantic retreats. In addition to a woodburning fireplace, each features a queen-sized canopied bed and a screened porch overlooking a lawn area. Room 1 has a small sitting room with a couch and is a bit larger. The bathroom has a tub and a shower. Our personal favorite, Room 2, has a bath with a tub-and-shower combination.

Rooms 3 and 4 (mid $100 range) are second-floor corners and each has a fireplace. The bathroom in Room 4 has a shower stall, while Room 3 has a bathroom with a painted wood floor and a tub-and-shower combination.

The entire third floor is given to Room 6 (low $100 range), which has a queen-sized pencil-post bed and a separate sitting room. There's also a small additional bedroom with a twin bed.

Room 5, a bargain for just over $100, faces the rear of the property and is decorated in blue and white tones. This chestnut-floored room features a queen-sized white-iron bed, a fluffy daybed, and a chaise longue. In the small bathroom, a clawfoot tub-and-shower combination sits under a window.

At the time of our visit, Milt and Gerrie were transforming a barn behind the house into a trio of spacious new guest rooms (mid to upper $100 range).

THE CAPTAIN'S HOUSE INN
OF CHATHAM

369-377 Old Harbor Road
Chatham, MA 02633
Telephone: (508) 945-0127

Sixteen rooms, each with private bath and telephone;
five with woodburning fireplaces. Amenities include
free rental bicycles and lawn croquet. Complimentary
full breakfast served at tables of two and four or in
your room. Complimentary tea and scones served
every afternoon. Handicapped access. Smoking is not
permitted. Two-night minimum stay required during
holiday periods. Moderate to expensive.

Getting There
From eastbound Route 6 on Cape Cod, take Route
137 to exit 11, then drive south to Route 28 and turn
left. At Chatham Center, follow the rotary out of
town on Route 28 toward Orleans for about one mile
to inn driveway on left.

THE CAPTAIN'S HOUSE INN
OF CHATHAM

Chatham

*I*t's unlikely that even Captain Hiram Harding, the privileged skipper who commissioned this patrician home, savored the romantic opulence available to guests today. It's more than a century and a half old, but there's little doubt that the Captain's House Inn is in finer shape today than the day it was completed.

Regarded consistently by respected lodging reviewers as the Cape's best-run hostelry, the inn owes its high standing to proprietors Dave and Jan McMaster, who continue to bestow loving attention on the gorgeous two-and-a-half-acre grounds and the charming vintage buildings.

Although they've been at the helm of the Captain's House only since 1993, the McMasters brought with them years of experience as the owners of a B&B near Oxford, England. In fact, the couple was drawn here by similarities between Chatham and Britain's small villages. Jan is a native of England and Dave is the founder and former chief executive of a computer company.

Guest accommodations at the Captain's House are spread among a main house, an adjacent two-hundred-year-old cottage with three rooms, and a renovated carriage house. Rooms are named after ships sailed by the original owner, and all have sitting areas, discreetly placed telephones, and air conditioning. Rates start in the lower $100 range.

Rooms for Romance

The most popular love nest is Hanna Rebecca, situated off the foyer of the main house in what used to function as a sitting room. This multiwindowed corner room (upper $100 range) with a floor of vintage pumpkin-pine holds a love seat, a working fireplace, and a queen-sized bed with a fishnet-style canopy. The bathroom, with a tub-and-shower combination, is tiny.

In our opinion, Eliza Jane, a rear corner room, is a bit too close to the dining room.

Of the three rooms in the Cape-style Captain's Cottage, Hiram Harding (around $200) is the most expensive. Features include pumpkin-pine plank floors, a large fireplace, a love seat, built-in bookshelves, and a white tiled bathroom with brass fixtures. Hideaway (upper $100 range) occupies the entire second floor and holds a tub and a separate shower for two.

In the carriage house, a rustic old wooden door opens to Whirlwind (high $100 range), a honeymoon-quality end unit with a private lawn and outdoor sitting area. Inside Tradewinds (high $100 range) is a large carriage house bedroom done in a wild bird motif. The room holds a beautiful queen-sized bed with a bow-shaped canopy. There's a combination tub-and-shower in the bathroom.

Similarly priced is Wild Pigeon, a lovely second-floor carriage house room with wood carpeting and a cathedral ceiling. A love seat is placed at the foot of a handsome canopied bed. There's also a tiny balcony.

THE INN AT WEST FALMOUTH

P.O. Box 1208
West Falmouth, MA 02574
Telephone: (508) 540-7696

Nine rooms, each with private bath; six with wood-burning fireplaces. Complimentary continental breakfast served at tables for two or in your room. Swimming pool and tennis court. Handicapped access. Smoking is not permitted. Two-night minimum stay required during weekends and holiday periods. Open all year. Expensive.

Getting There
The inn is located off Highway 28A and Blacksmith Shop Road in West Falmouth. The innkeeper prefers to provide specific driving instructions after confirming reservations.

THE INN AT WEST FALMOUTH

West Falmouth

*E*ven in a locale as famous and well traveled as Cape Cod, a few secrets remain. The Inn at West Falmouth, which lies hidden and unmarked at the end of a narrow wooded gravel lane well off the beaten path, is quite possibly the cape's most romantic destination.

From the outside, the shingled home oozes classic nineteenth-century New England charm. The interior, however, has been completely redone to reflect the appealing romantic vision of innkeeper Lewis Milardo.

Lewis and a business associate, who happened upon the long-neglected turn-of-the-century summer cottage a few years ago, removed walls to create nine stunning suites and rooms, built sumptuous and spacious marble-floored bathrooms, installed intriguing windows and woodburning fireplaces, and added a number of cozy balconies with garden and Buzzards Bay views. A small swimming pool and tennis court are the crowning touches.

Located only about fifteen minutes from the Woods Hole ferry terminal, the inn is a perfect resting place for Martha's Vineyard–bound travelers.

Rooms for Romance

Guest quarters exude a romantically eclectic aura. Your room might combine colorful chintz with an antique Oriental chest, or a Moroccan rug with luxurious Waverly fabric.

The best view in the house is offered from the third floor in Room 8 (high $100 range), where two comfortable chairs are placed before a large bay-view window. A queen-sized bed sits under a multi-angled ceiling.

Room 6 (mid $100 range) is a very private second-floor corner hideaway with a canopied queen-sized bed and a tiny bay-view balcony with a couple of chairs.

We spent an enchanting summer night in Room 3 (high $100 range), a spacious suite featuring a sitting nook with cushioned window seat, a fireplace, a canopied, four-poster queen-sized bed, and a large pool- and bay-view balcony with a comfortable chaise and chair set.

Room 6 is equipped with a double bed and rooms 7 and 9 have twin beds. Rooms 1, 3, 5, and 7 have woodburning fireplaces. These rooms are offered in the mid to upper $100 range.

Among the indulgent romantic amenities provided for guests are a tiny observation tower with a telescope, crisply ironed sheets, six pillows for each bed, and fresh flowers. Traveling couples who savor privacy will also enjoy the innkeeper's unobtrusive style as well as tables for two on the deck and in the dining room.

THE CHARLOTTE INN

27 South Summer Street
Edgartown, MA 02539
Telephone: (508) 627-4151

Twenty-five rooms, each with private bath; five
with woodburning fireplaces. L'étoile restaurant.
Handicapped access. Smoking is allowed. Two-night
minimum stay required during most weekends in
season; three-night minimum during holiday periods.
Deluxe.

Getting There
From the Oak Bluffs ferry dock, drive south on
Seaview Avenue, which becomes Beach Road, then
Edgartown-Oak Bluffs Road, and finally Main Street
in Edgartown. Turn right on Summer Street and fol-
low to inn on left. For ferry reservations, contact the
Steamship Authority at (508) 477-8600.

THE CHARLOTTE INN

Edgartown

*I*n our Vineyard wanderings, we've failed to discover a more enchanting community than Edgartown. And we can't imagine a finer romantic complement to an overnight Edgartown visit than a guest room at this sublime inn.

Set at the heart of town and spread among a collection of fine buildings that run from patrician to quaint, the inn is well positioned for tours not only of Edgartown, but also the island. It's also a short walk to the harbor and the Chappaquiddick ferry.

The compound's centerpiece is a mid-nineteenth-century whaling merchant's home. The lower level holds the registration area, grand parlors, and an open and airy dining room. Winding walkways, hidden gardens, and patios offer visiting couples lots of opportunities for private outdoor enjoyment.

Rooms for Romance

Of the seven rooms in the main house, Room 12 ($400 range) is one of the romantics' choices. Features include a canopied four-poster bed, a woodburning fireplace, and a separate sitting area. Rooms 9 and 10, (around $250), are among the inn's less expensive accommodations. These smaller rooms have double beds. You'll need to invest at least around $325 in-season for a room with a queen-sized bed.

Next door is Summer House, the former residence of a sea captain that now houses seven guest rooms. The lower-level rooms face a long covered porch overlooking an exquisitely sculpted lawn and garden area. A grand piano occupies Room 14 (mid $400 range), which also has a fireplace and a sitting area.

At the rear of the property stands a two-story refurbished carriage house whose rooms are among the inn's most secluded. Room 2 (around $300) is a small, handsome hideaway with deep green carpeting, English antiques, a queen-sized four-poster bed, and a love seat. It also boasts a private lawn and garden area.

Directly across the tree-lined street from the main building is Garden House, which dates from 1705. There are six comfortable rooms here. Room 20, priced at around $250, is the least expensive.

High-season rates (from early June through early October) at the Charlotte Inn are among the island's most expensive. However, nightly rates at other times of the year are as much as $100 cheaper.

Visitors should be aware that traffic can be a problem in Edgartown, and guests may have to park three blocks away from the inn.

THORNCROFT INN

278 Main Street
Vineyard Haven, MA 02568-1022
Telephone: (508) 693-3333

Thirteen rooms, each with private bath; nine with woodburning fireplaces; four with hot tubs for two. Complimentary full breakfast served at tables for two or larger. No handicapped access. Smoking is not permitted. Two-night minimum stay required during weekends; three-night minimum during holiday periods. Expensive to deluxe.

Getting There

From the Vineyard Haven ferry dock, turn right at the stop sign and turn right on Main Street. Drive one mile to inn on left. From the Oak Bluffs ferry dock, follow signs to Vineyard Haven and turn right on Main Street. Drive one mile to inn on left. For ferry reservations, contact the Steamship Authority at (508) 477-8600.

THORNCROFT INN

Vineyard Haven

*O*n this romantic island that appears to have been created especially for lovers, there's a seemingly endless list of places to go and things to see and do together. Therein lies the essence of what we call the Thorncroft dilemma. This lovely inn is almost too difficult to leave, even for a few hours of Vineyard exploration. Not only do we rank Thorncroft Inn as the island's preeminent lodging choice, we consider it one of the finest and most romantic destinations in all of New England.

Rooms for Romance

One of the most romantic features we've yet discovered in our travels is found in both rooms 1 and 10 (mid $300 range). Guests here are treated to three-hundred-gallon hot tubs that are so big they're housed in completely private adjoining rooms.

Warm water experiences are also available in rooms 9 and 14 (around $300) where ninety-gallon spa tubs for two are placed in mirrored bedroom alcoves.

Our generous slice of heaven, Room 12 (mid to upper $200 range) on the second floor of the remote Carriage House, was reached by a lighted gravel path through a dense growth of trees and brush at the rear of the property. The centerpiece of this large corner room was a raised queen-sized bed with a fishnet canopy. A marble fireplace was prepared and needed only a match. Walls were papered tastefully, and windows and walls were trimmed in stained pine. French doors opened onto a private balcony with chairs overlooking a side lawn. The bath was compact, holding a tub-and-shower combination.

Rooms in the main house—there are eight of these—have wireless headphones for TV watching, a thoughtful feature that ensures a quiet romantic atmosphere. Main house room rates range from the high $100 range to the mid $300 range. Off-season rates (early September through mid-June) are considerably less expensive than tariffs noted here.

At the time of our visit, innkeepers Karl and Lynn Buder had plans in hand for yet another collection of decadently romantic rooms in which more happy couples will face the Thorncroft dilemma.

CLIFFSIDE BEACH CLUB

P.O. Box 449
Nantucket, MA 02554
Telephone: (508) 228-0618

Twenty-eight rooms, suites, and cottages, each with
private bath. Complimentary continental breakfast
served in lobby or in your room. Private swimming
beach with umbrellas, chairs, and towels. Exercise
room and restaurant. No handicapped access.
Smoking is allowed. Four-night minimum stay during
high-season only. Closed during winter. Deluxe.

Getting There
Nantucket Island is served by ferry from the Massachusetts mainland and by air from various points.
For car/passenger ferry reservations, contact the
Steamship Authority at (508) 540-2022. The Hy-Line,
which provides swifter, passenger-only ferry transport,
can be reached by calling (508) 778-2600. The beach
club will arrange transportation from the Nantucket
ferry dock and airport.

CLIFFSIDE BEACH CLUB

Nantucket

The contemporary accommodations of Cliffside Beach Club strike quite a contrast to the older, more traditional bed-and-breakfast inns we passed on the way to the beach. This is Nantucket at its most indulgent.

Set right on the sand facing the Atlantic, Cliffside is the island's only exclusive beach resort. If water, sand, and sun fire your romantic notions, you've come to the right place.

New England old-timers might recall when this was an exclusive members-only resort, where marked and reserved spaces on the sand had everything to do with social standing and tradition. While still a private club, the property has lost its 1950s and 1960s stuffiness; nonmember guests are now warmly welcomed and comfortably accommodated in new and refurbished units ranging from hotel rooms and studios to spacious cottages.

Our springtime visit to Nantucket coincided with an unusual several-week-long warm spell, and the beach club, bathed in golden sunshine, was in its glory. There being precious few vacancies, we were only able to tour a couple of units, but what we saw was impressive.

Rooms for Romance

Accommodations at Cliffside are situated against the busier main beach or on the quieter Gold Coast section of beach on the east side. High-season rates (late June through Labor Day weekend) run from the low to mid $200 range for a hotel-type room to the upper $500 range for a cottage.

The exteriors are typical Nantucket: weathered shingles and white trim. Step inside and you'll be greeted by contemporary freshness and amenities, including fine woodwork by local artisans. Angled wainscoting figures prominently in the interior design, and beds are contained in matching angled wood frames.

One of the favorite choices among romantics, Room 205, is actually one of the resort's least expensive, fetching rates from around $200 to the mid $200 range, depending on the season. This unit, classified as a hotel room, has an angled water view.

Other popular romantic accommodations are beachfront studios 201 through 204 and deck rooms 122 through 127. All are offered from the lower $200 range to the high $300 range, depending on time of year.

Most rooms have queen-sized beds. Cottage 210 has a fireplace. Rooms 206, 207, and 208 do not have water views.

It may be one of our most expensive featured hideaways, but Cliffside Beach Club isn't necessarily out of the reach of economically minded romantics. One option is to visit during the club's low season (late May through early June and late September through early October) when hotel units and studio apartments are available from the mid $100 range. You might also consider traveling with another couple or two and share the cost of a multibedroomed apartment.

CONNECTICUT

DAYTIME DIVERSIONS

Deep River, one of our featured destinations, is only a short drive from Mystic and Hammonassett Beach. The romance of a nineteenth-century coastal village is preserved at Mystic Seaport, one of New England's most popular attractions.

The scenic roads of wondrous Litchfield Hills will transport you past rural farms and quaint villages, and to antique stores, galleries, and romantic outdoor places.

From the old stone tower on Haystack Mountain near Norfolk you can see the Berkshires and all the way to Long Island Sound.

In Ridgefield, hiking trails are accessible directly from Stonehenge Inn's property. Steeprock Reserve near the Mayflower Inn is another favorite destination for hikers.

The Boulders has private lake access as well as ping pong, free rental boats, and windsurfing boards. Nearby New Preston is a tiny village with a handful of interesting shops.

TABLES FOR TWO

The Boulders, described in this section, has its own
  highly rated dining room
The West Street Grill, West Street, Litchfield
Mountain View Inn, Route 272, Norfolk
Bravo Bravo, 18 Eiman Street, Mystic
The Cannery, Main Street, Canaan
Under Mountain Inn, 482 Under Mountain Road,
  Route 41, Salisbury

MANOR HOUSE

69 Maple Avenue
Norfolk, CT 06058
Telephone: (203) 542-5690

Nine rooms, each with private bath; two with wood-burning fireplaces. Complimentary full breakfast served at a communal table or in your room. No handicapped access. Smoking is not permitted. Two-night minimum stay required during weekends and holiday periods. Moderate to expensive.

Getting There
From Boston, exit the Massachusetts Turnpike (Interstate 90) at Route 7 and drive south. At Canaan, take Route 44 east to Norfolk. Turn left on Maple Avenue and follow to inn on left. From New York, follow Interstate 84 to Route 8 north at Waterbury, CT. At terminus of highway (Winstead), take Route 44 west and follow to Norfolk. Turn right on Maple Avenue and follow to inn on left.

MANOR HOUSE

Norfolk

*L*ike crunching leaves on an autumn stroll, a soft breeze on a summer night, or a warming fire during a snowfall, Manor House adds just the right touch to a romantic weekend away.

One of our favorite New England destinations, this nine-room property strikes an engaging balance between a tiny bed-and-breakfast inn and a small hotel. Boasting a storybook Bavarian Tudor façade, the mansion was exquisitely crafted just before the turn of the twentieth century by Charles Spofford, architect of London's subway system. The artful stained-glass windows that still illuminate the public areas were a housewarming gift from famed glass craftsman Louis Tiffany.

Rooms for Romance

Don't worry about being assigned a room off the kitchen or parlor; all of the antique-furnished guest quarters are tucked privately away on the second and third floors. One of the most romantic is the English Room (mid to upper $100 range), a bright corner on the second floor with a king-sized bed and the most sumptuous bathroom in the house. Its centerpiece is a two-person spa tub set against windows and under a ceiling fan. The sink is set inside an antique dresser.

The beautifully windowed Spofford Room (mid $100 range) holds a fireplace, a sitting area, and a king-sized canopied bed. The bathroom has a shower, and there's a private backyard-view balcony with wicker furnishings.

Another of our most highly recommended hideaways is the third-floor Country French Room (mid $100 range). Featuring a coffered ceiling and tasteful wallpaper, the room overlooks the inn's backyard. The tiled bath, which holds a large soaking tub for two, is paneled in cedar and lit by a skylight.

The inn's most private room is the third-floor Chalet Suite (low $100 range), reached by a private stairway. Situated under the eaves, the suite has a bedroom with a queen-sized antique spool bed, and a sitting area with a day bed. There's a shower stall under a skylight in the suite's tiny bathroom.

Commanding a very competitive rate of around $100, La Chambre, which was in need of a carpet upgrade at the time of our visit, has a queen-sized brass and iron bed, two wing chairs, and a windowed bathroom with a clawfoot tub-and-shower combination.

We do not recommend the Victorian Room for romantic getaways only because its private bathroom is located down the hall.

THE BOULDERS

Route 45, East Shore Road
New Preston, CT 06777
Telephone: (203) 868-0541

Seventeen rooms, each with private bath; eleven with woodburning fireplaces. Complimentary full breakfast served at tables for two in the dining room or in your room. Handicapped access. Smoking is allowed. Two-night minimum stay required during weekends; three-night minimum during holiday periods. Expensive to deluxe.

Getting There
From Boston, follow the Massachusetts Turnpike (Interstate 90) west to Route 84, the Sturbridge exit. Follow Route 84 west to Farmington; then follow Route 4 and Route 118 to Litchfield; take Route 202 to New Preston. Turn right on Route 45 and follow to Lake Waramaug. At the lake, veer right and drive along East Shore Road for one mile to inn on right. From New York, follow Highway 684 north to Route 84, and east to Route 7. Follow Route 7 north, then Route 202 north to New Preston. Turn right on Route 45 and follow to Lake Waramaug. At the lake, veer right and drive along East Shore Road for one mile to inn on right.

THE BOULDERS

New Preston

For you, there's nothing like a view of the water; unfortunately, your partner's inspired by a mountain vista. Not to worry. A mutually satisfying romantic weekend awaits at this cozy inn along the banks of Lake Waramaug in the Berkshire Hills of northwestern Connecticut. From your enchanting base at the Boulders, you can hike or ski the trails of majestic Pinnacle Mountain in the morning and paddle the afternoon away on the lake.

A magical marriage of water and woods, the Boulders is a refurbished hundred-year-old estate that during its early years hosted the well-to-do of New England.

The main house, which playfully mixes gambrels, dormers, shingles, angles, and stone, is the centerpiece of the property, which slopes from the base of the hills to the lake. The inn's living area, full of couches and cozy nooks, is paneled in knotty pine, reminiscent of a comfortable mountain retreat. In warmer weather, many guests can be found relaxing or dining on the many patios that overlook the lake.

The Boulders doesn't simply offer views of Lake Waramaug; visitors have full access to the lake. A private boathouse, maintained for guest use, has paddleboats, canoes, rowboats, and windsurfing equipment, as well as lounge furniture for those who prefer to loll on the grassy shore.

Rooms for Romance

To make the most of your romantic visit to the Boulders, we strongly recommend booking one of the many rooms with a view of the beautiful lake just across the road.

In the main house, four rooms (high $100 range) on the second floor face the water. Among these is Southwest, a corner room with a queen-sized canopied iron bed and a small lake-view balcony. The bathroom contains a shower stall. Northwest, another sunny corner, has a lake-view window seat. You'll even catch a peek of the lake from the room's king-sized bed.

The two suites in the main house (around $200), while offering separate sitting areas, do not have inspiring lake vistas.

For more privacy and space, guests may opt for one of the duplex guest houses (high $100 range to mid $200 range) set among mature trees above the main house. These have shaded private decks, fireplaces, and refrigerators, and all have picture-window views of the lake. Nugget South and North (mid $200 range) have spa tubs for two. Cobble is the most remote cottage; Gem North is a sunny unit offering a stunning lake view not at all obscured by trees.

Another building, the recently constructed Carriage House, contains three luxurious rooms (around $200), all of which have fireplaces.

The rates noted above are for bed and breakfast. For an additional charge of around $50, a couple may visit on a modified American plan and enjoy dinner in the inn's romantic dining room or on the lake-view deck.

THE MAYFLOWER INN

Route 47
Washington, CT 06793
Telephone: (203) 868-9466

Twenty-five rooms and suites, each with private bath;
fourteen with gas fireplaces. Heated swimming pool,
tennis court, and fitness facility. Restaurant and
lounge. Handicapped access. Smoking is discouraged
but allowed. Two-night minimum stay required during weekends; three-night minimum during holiday
periods. Deluxe.

Getting There
From Boston, take the Massachusetts Turnpike
(Interstate 90) to Interstate 84; take 84 west to
Southbury (exit 15). Turn right on Route 6 north
and drive five miles to the stop light and Route 47
road sign. Turn left and follow Route 47 for eight
miles to Washington. Directions from New York
City (a two-hour drive) are available from the inn
on request.

THE MAYFLOWER INN

Washington

*A*fter sitting closed and neglected for many years, this private-school-turned-inn transcended its original luster in the early 1990s through some serious attention by Adriana and Robert Mnuchin. The new owners imported European antiques, created spacious marbled bathrooms, installed buttery canopied beds, and restored more than two dozen luscious acres to create a radiant lovers' sanctuary. This is quite possibly southern New England's loveliest inn.

Rooms for Romance

We're hard pressed to choose between the inn's three separate buildings. The stunning main house, called Mayflower, holds fifteen rooms and suites as well as the inn's dining room and fitness facilities. We were impressed with Room 27 (low to mid $200 range) on the second floor, from which guests have pretty views of gardens and lawn. Furnishings include a king-sized canopied bed, an armoire with a television, and a writing desk. The bathroom holds a deep tub for two and a separate shower stall. This is among the Mayflower's least expensive accommodations.

In the five-room Speedwell building, Room 10 (low to mid $300 range) features a private balcony in addition to a king-sized canopied bed and a fireplace. For a few dollars more, the two of you may savor Room 15, a small Speedwell suite with a large balcony, a full living room, a fireplace, and a spa tub for two. The nearby Standish building holds five more rooms and suites.

At the time of our visit, the Mayflower Inn posted a generous and romantically sensitive check-out time of 1 p.m.

STONEHENGE INN
AND RESTAURANT

Route 7
Ridgefield, CT 06877
Telephone: (203) 438-6511

Sixteen rooms and suites, each with private bath.
Complimentary full breakfast served in your room.
Swimming pool, restaurant. Handicapped access.
Smoking is allowed. No minimum night stay require-
ment. Moderate to deluxe.

Getting There
From Interstate 95, midway between New York City
and New Haven, take exit 15 and drive north on
Route 7 past Ridgefield to the inn's drive on left. The
inn is approximately five miles south of Danbury and
thirteen miles north of Merritt Parkway (Route 15).
Driving distance from New York is approximately
55 miles. Boston is approximately 180 miles away.

STONEHENGE INN AND RESTAURANT

Ridgefield

*I*f the number of on-site weddings and anniversary celebrations is any gauge of a destination's romantic potential, Stonehenge Inn and Restaurant must rank among Connecticut's top choices. Nary a weekend goes by here without some type of grand or intimate celebration of romance. In fact, on the weekend of our visit, the entire property had been taken over by a wedding party.

The wiles of Stonehenge begin working their romantic magic as you leave the highway and follow the driveway through one of New England's picture-perfect properties. Many weddings take place adjacent to the inn's lovely lake, which is also home to graceful swans. Deer also tiptoe out of the peripheral forest from time to time to stroll about the expansive property, developed as an inn back in the 1940s.

Rooms for Romance

The grounds of Stonehenge are extraordinary, but we found the accommodations somewhat less inspired than those in most of our other destinations.

Traditional early American furnishings decorate the inn's sixteen guest rooms, which are scattered among three Colonial-style buildings. There are six rooms in the main lodge, six more in a single-level T-shaped guest cottage, and four units in a guest house at the rear of the property.

A number of celebrities have sought romantic refuge in Devon and Kent (around $200), the apartment-sized suites on the ground floor of the remote guest house, our personal favorite. Surrey and Cornwall (mid to upper $100 range), on the upper level, are spacious chambers with king-sized beds and sitting areas furnished with couches.

In the main building, which also houses the inn's restaurant, York (mid $100 range) is a charming, smaller room with a queen-sized four-poster bed. Least expensive are the somewhat tired, king-bedded rooms of the guest cottage, offered in the low to mid $100 range.

RIVERWIND INN

209 Main Street
Deep River, CT 06417
Telephone: (203) 526-2014

Eight rooms, each with private bath. Complimentary
full breakfast served at a communal table and tables
for two or taken to your room. Smoking is allowed.
Two-night minimum stay required during weekends
from April through December and during holiday
weekends. Moderate to expensive.

Getting There
From Interstate 95 at Old Saybrook, follow Route 9
north to exit 4, then follow Route 154 for one and a
half miles to Deep River. The inn is on Main Street.

RIVERWIND INN

Deep River

Traveling couples who share a love of Americana will revel in this museum-quality inn, one of the most unusual destinations we've sampled in New England.

From floor to ceiling, every nook and cranny of the two-story home is crammed with a fascinating assortment of American antiques and bric-a-brac, all collected by innkeepers Bob Bucknall and Barbara Barlow, who continue to prowl antique stores in search of more. Some guests may find Riverwind cluttered and excessive; others will consider it a whimsical delight.

Constructed in the early 1800s as a private residence, the home was faithfully restored by Barbara, who discovered it abandoned in the early 1980s. Bob later doubled the inn's guest capacity, adding four romantic guest rooms that hold true to the structure's nineteenth-century appearance.

We aren't particularly impressed with the community of Deep River as a romantic destination, but the little village does serve as a convenient base for Connecticut River valley explorations.

Rooms for Romance

Willow (low $100 range), a newer ground-floor room, is one of our three romantic favorites. Furnished with an antique canopied four-poster bed and a wing chair, Willow boasts a small private deck overlooking the inn's backyard.

On the second floor, Champagne and Roses (mid $100 range), another of the more recent room additions, is a bright and spacious rear corner that features windows on three sides and two wing chairs. There's also a private deck set among the branches of a backyard tree. The bathroom holds a shower stall and a deep soaking tub into which two people might squeeze. The queen-sized bed is partially canopied and sits under a ceiling fan.

Another top choice is the plank-floored Zelda's (low to mid $100 range), a two-room suite where an antique oak bed is set below a row of small, six-over-six windows. There's a brass daybed in a windowless sitting room. The bathroom has a tub-and-shower combination.

The Havlow Room has a private bath, but it's located down the hall a few steps. The Barn Rose Room is a bit too close to the inn's public areas for our romantic tastes, and at the time of our visit it looked a bit tired.

STEAMBOAT INN

73 Steamboat Wharf
Mystic, CT 06355
Telephone: (203) 536-8300

Ten rooms, each with private bath; six with fireplaces; five with tubs for two. Complimentary continental breakfast served at tables for two or in your room. Handicapped access. Smoking is not permitted. Two-night minimum stay required during weekends. Moderate to deluxe.

Getting There

From Interstate 95 northbound, take exit 89 and turn right on Allyn Street. Turn left on West Main Street (second traffic light) and follow to inn on right, just before the drawbridge. Park in the adjacent public lot. From southbound Interstate 95, take exit 90 and turn left on Route 27. Turn right on Route 1 (Main Street) and drive to inn on left just past the drawbridge. Park in the adjacent public lot.

STEAMBOAT INN

Mystic

*D*on't be put off by the anonymous entrance from a public parking lot. The real mystique of Mystic unfolds once inside your romantic guest room.

Occupying a coveted village spot along the Mystic River just off Main Street, Steamboat Inn is a modern, two-story hostelry with large, generously windowed, stylishly decorated rooms along with luxurious bathrooms. Half of the rooms have whirlpool tubs for two; six feature woodburning fireplaces.

Despite its central location within walking distance of Mystic attractions, restaurants, and boutiques, the inn offers surprising peace and quiet, even during the bustling daytime hours. Evenings often find guests curled up in their guest room windows watching the parade of pleasure boats pass by only a few yards away.

In the morning, breakfast is served informally from the bar of a second-floor "gathering room" with a black-and-white checkerboard floor. Guests sit at tables for two.

Rooms for Romance

Guest rooms feature unusual angles and each is individually styled; you won't be greeted by standard, cookie-cutter arrangements here.

Kathleen (mid $200 range), the room we stayed in, was a spacious abode holding a king-sized canopied bed. French doors opened to a separate sitting room with a couch, a chair, and an armoire that held a television. The wainscoted bathroom held a spa tub for two and a separate shower stall. During our visit, a vintage schooner was moored just outside the window.

Ariadne (high $100 range) is the inn's designated honeymoon room. Located on the second floor, it boasts a sweeping harbor view, a canopied bed, a love seat facing a fireplace, and a spa tub for two in the bathroom. Ariadne is the only second-floor room with a spa tub for two.

Similarly priced is Mystic, a second-floor corner with wraparound windows. A view of the fireplace and harbor is offered from the four-poster bed. The small bathroom holds an individual-sized whirlpool bath/shower combination.

The Annie Wilcox room (mid $100 range) holds two double beds.

We didn't find an undesirable guest chamber in the inn, but because of occasional foot traffic along a harbor walk that runs past the downstairs windows, couples in these rooms will need to draw the drapes and sacrifice the river view for complete privacy. For this reason, we prefer the inn's upstairs rooms, where a private harbor view will surely enhance your intimate experiences.

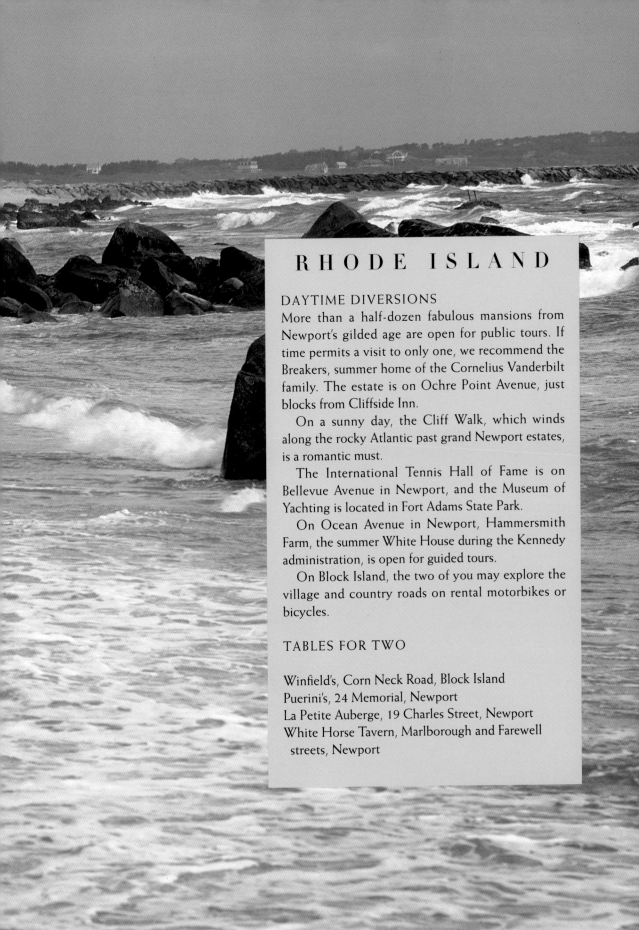

RHODE ISLAND

DAYTIME DIVERSIONS

More than a half-dozen fabulous mansions from Newport's gilded age are open for public tours. If time permits a visit to only one, we recommend the Breakers, summer home of the Cornelius Vanderbilt family. The estate is on Ochre Point Avenue, just blocks from Cliffside Inn.

On a sunny day, the Cliff Walk, which winds along the rocky Atlantic past grand Newport estates, is a romantic must.

The International Tennis Hall of Fame is on Bellevue Avenue in Newport, and the Museum of Yachting is located in Fort Adams State Park.

On Ocean Avenue in Newport, Hammersmith Farm, the summer White House during the Kennedy administration, is open for guided tours.

On Block Island, the two of you may explore the village and country roads on rental motorbikes or bicycles.

TABLES FOR TWO

Winfield's, Corn Neck Road, Block Island
Puerini's, 24 Memorial, Newport
La Petite Auberge, 19 Charles Street, Newport
White Horse Tavern, Marlborough and Farewell
  streets, Newport

CLIFFSIDE INN

2 Seaview Avenue
Newport, RI 02840
Telephone: (401) 847-1811 or
toll-free: (800) 845-1811

Thirteen rooms, each with private bath; five with woodburning fireplaces; five with tubs for two. Complimentary full breakfast served in dining room at communal table. No handicapped access. Smoking is not permitted. Two-night minimum stay required during weekends; two- or three-night minimum during holiday periods. Expensive to deluxe.

Getting There

From Interstate 195 at Fall River, MA, follow Route 24 south to Route 114 south. Route 114 becomes West Main Road in Newport. Turn left on Valley Road (Route 214) and follow south as Valley Road curves right onto Memorial Boulevard. From Memorial Boulevard, turn left on Cliff Avenue and left on Seaview Avenue to inn on left.

# CLIFFSIDE INN

Newport

The many paintings of Beatrice Turner, a beautiful heiress whose family resided long ago in what is now Cliffside Inn, convey a haunting romantic quality to this eclectic Victorian. Sadly, romance was apparently missing from Beatrice's lonely life. As evidenced by her personal diary and scores of self-portraits, many of which line the stairwell and public rooms, Beatrice was self-obsessed, leading the life of a reclusive artist after the death of her parents.

Built in 1880 as a summer getaway for the governor of Maryland, the mansion passed to the Turner family at the turn of the century. It was in these grand rooms that Beatrice painted more than one thousand portraits of herself and her family. Although much of the artwork was destroyed after Beatrice's death in the late 1940s, the surviving paintings speak volumes about the artist's life, from radiant youth to tragically lonely middle age.

Romance may have eluded the previous owner, but it pervades the Cliffside today. This informal and genial inn is not only an ideal base from which to explore all of Newport's charms, it's a great place to simply cozy up with someone special.

One of Cliffside's great romantic assets is direct access to Newport's famous Cliff Walk, where the two of you can stroll along the Atlantic past grand mansions from the gilded age. Cornelius Vanderbilt's magnificent Breakers and other neighboring estates are open for tours and are just a few blocks from the inn.

Rooms for Romance

The most popular room is Miss Beatrice's (low to mid $200 range) on the second floor. It's a spacious chamber with a queen-sized bed, a woodburning fireplace, and a bay window seat. In the bathroom is a spa tub for two set in a bay window and, for your romantic pleasure, a separate shower with dual fixtures.

Our personal favorite lovers' lair is the Governor's Suite (low $300 range), a bright third-floor space equipped with a love seat, a king-sized four-poster bed, and a two-sided fireplace. The bathroom, one of the most indulgent we've seen in New England, is a warm-water fantasyland, holding a whirlpool tub as well as a one-of-a-kind antique Victorian "bird cage" shower with a sensual full-body, total-surround spray.

Our night here was spent in the Turner Suite (low to mid $200 range), also high on the third floor. A handsome antique queen-sized bed was covered with a spread whose floral print matched its canopy and bedside lamp shades. The romantic bathroom, with a black-and-white tiled floor, contained a large spa tub for two equipped with a hand-held shower attachment. A separate skylit sitting room, located between the bed and bathroom, held a love seat, a dressing table, and bookshelves.

The Veranda Room (mid $100 range), with Laura Ashley decor and a queen-sized bed, is situated off the front porch and has a private outside entry. This is one of the inn's least expensive rooms. All rooms here have air conditioning, televisions, and telephones.

THE FRANCIS MALBONE HOUSE

392 Thames Street
Newport, RI 02840
Telephone: (401) 846-0392

Nine rooms, each with private bath; six with woodburning fireplaces. Complimentary full breakfast
served in dining room at communal table. No handicapped access. Smoking is not permitted. Two-night
minimum stay required during weekends; three-night
minimum during holiday periods. Expensive to deluxe.

Getting There
From Interstate 195 at Fall River, MA, follow Route
24 south to Route 114 south. Route 114 becomes
West Main Road in Newport. Turn left on Valley
Road (Route 214) and follow south as Valley Road
curves right onto Memorial Boulevard. From Memorial
Boulevard at the harbor, turn left on Lower Thames
Street and follow to inn on left.

THE FRANCIS MALBONE HOUSE

Newport

*I*n Newport, our two recommended destinations capture delightfully different moods: the quiet, well-established neighborhood environs of Cliffside Inn or the lively harbor-village setting of the Francis Malbone House.

Harbor shops and attractions are literally a few steps away from the Malbone House, but the fast pace of the village slows to a pleasant crawl inside this charming Colonial home, built in the mid-1700s for a prominent shipping merchant.

Boasting a glistening, creamy colored brick façade, this handsome inn belies its age of over two hundred years. The interior is likewise fresh and elegant, with four parlors and two living rooms providing many quiet corners for traveling romantics. A well-tended and comfortable backyard garden, another of the inn's pleasing features, serves as a relaxing haven after a day of combing the bustling village.

Rooms for Romance

Rooms are classified as either harbor view (around $200) or garden view (mid $100 range). The Counting House Suite is available for around $300.

One of the nicest harbor views is offered from the several windows of Room 3 on the second floor. This front-facing corner holds a queen-sized four-poster bed and a fireplace. The bathroom has a shower stall.

A similar vista is available from Room 6 on the third floor, where even the bathroom has a water view. This room, with wide plank floors, has a queen-sized four-poster bed, two wing chairs, and a fireplace.

Among the charming garden view rooms is Room 8, a small rear-facing unit with a queen-sized bed and one chair. The bathroom has a tub-and-shower combination.

NICHOLAS BALL COTTAGE

1 Spring Street (Hotel Manisses address)
Block Island, RI 02807
Telephone: (401) 466-2421 or (401) 466-2063

Three cottage rooms, each with private bath, spa tub
for two, and fireplace. Complimentary full breakfast
served at tables for two in dining room of adjacent
1661 Inn. No handicapped access. Smoking is allowed.
Call for multi-night stay requirements. Expensive to
deluxe.

Getting There
From Interstate 95 at East Greenwich, follow Route 4
south, to Route 1 south, to Point Judith exit. Follow
signs to Block Island ferry. Call (401) 783-4613 for
ferry reservations. Taxi service to the inn is available
at the Block Island ferry landing.

NICHOLAS BALL COTTAGE

Block Island

$\mathcal{E}$ ven for a couple of veteran ferry riders like ourselves, a few miles of ocean still does wonders to clear the mind and enliven the romantic spirit. It's especially true when the destination is as tasty as Nicholas Ball Cottage, an island secret we only begrudgingly share.

The cottage, which is actually a replica of an old Episcopal church destroyed long ago by a hurricane, is operated by the owners of Hotel Manisses, a Block Island landmark, and the 1661 Inn, which stands next door to the cottage. We did not tour the hotel or inn.

Guests needn't transport their cars to the island as the cottage is only a short walk from the ferry dock. Taxi service is available, and motorized scooters may be rented for island exploring. Restaurants, shops, and beaches are also within walking distance of the cottage.

Rooms for Romance

Situated on an ocean bluff, the cottage has three luxurious rooms that are delightful in every respect. Cassius is a two-story, nicely windowed, front-facing suite with wool carpeting. The downstairs bed chamber is furnished with two chairs, an antique dressing table, and a desk. The bathroom is equipped with a large shower stall. The romantic loft holds an oval spa tub for two set under two dormer windows with peeks of the ocean. There's also a couch and a tiled fireplace.

Colfax, which is next door, has a similar arrangement and the same amenities, and is decorated in pink tones.

The Nicholas Room is a spacious, single-level room with a king-sized canopy bed, a tiled fireplace, a fainting couch, and a large step-up spa tub for two set under beautiful windows. This room does not offer an ocean view.

Cottage room rates vary wildly, depending on the time of your visit. The lowest rates (mid $100 range) are, as you might expect, available during the winter months. The highest rates (mid to high $200 range) are commanded from July through Labor Day weekend.

INDEX